W9-ARK-209

STEVEN SPIELBERG

★ ★ ★ ★ ★ ★ ★ ★ ★ ★ ★ ★ ★ ★ ★ ★ ★ ★

POP CULTURE LEGENDS

STEVEN SPIELBERG

★ ★

ELIZABETH FERBER

CHELSEA HOUSE PUBLISHERS

★ Philadelphia ★

CHELSEA HOUSE PUBLISHERS

EDITORIAL DIRECTOR Rick Rennert
PICTURE EDITOR Judy Hasday
ART DIRECTOR Sara Davis
PRODUCTION MANAGER Pamela Loos

Staff for STEVEN SPIELBERG
SENIOR EDITORS Kathy Kuhtz Campbell, Jane Shumate
ASSOCIATE EDITOR Therese De Angelis
EDITORIAL ASSISTANT Kristine Brennan
SENIOR DESIGNER Cambraia Magalhaes
PICTURE RESEARCHER Ellen Barrett Dudley
COVER ILLUSTRATOR Daniel O'Leary

First Printing
  1 3 5 7 9 8 6 4 2

Library of Congress Cataloging-in-Publication Data
Ferber, Elizabeth, 1967–
Steven Spielberg: a biography / by Elizabeth Ferber.
    p. cm. —(Pop culture legends).
Includes bibliographical references and index.
ISBN 0-7910-3256-6
        0-7910-3257-4 (pbk.)
1. Spielberg, Steven, 1947- —Juvenile literature. 2. Motion
picture producers and directors—United States—
Biography—Juvenile literature. I. Title. II. Series
PN1998.3.S65F47 1996   95-41571
791.43'0233'092—dc20   CIP

FRONTISPIECE:
Steven Spielberg during production of *Schindler's List*, the
film that finally married his technical wizardry with emotional and dramatic depth, winning him twin Oscars in
1993.

Contents ★ ★ ★ ★ ★ ★ ★ ★ ★ ★ ★ ★ ★ ★ ★ ★ ★ ★

A Reflection of Ourselves

Leeza Gibbons

I ENJOY A RARE PERSPECTIVE on the entertainment industry. From my window on popular culture, I can see all that sizzles and excites. I have interviewed legends who have left us, such as Bette Davis and Sammy Davis, Jr., and have brushed shoulders with the names who have caused a commotion with their sheer outrageousness, like Boy George and Madonna. Whether it's by nature or by design, pop icons generate interest, and I think they are a mirror of who we are at any given time.

Who are *your* heroes and heroines, the people you most admire? Outside of your own family and friends, to whom do you look for inspiration and guidance, as examples of the type of person you would like to be as an adult? How do we decide who will be the most popular and influential members of our society?

You may be surprised by your answers. According to recent polls, you will probably respond much differently than your parents or grandparents did to the same questions at the same age. Increasingly, world leaders such as Winston Churchill, John F. Kennedy, Franklin D. Roosevelt, and evangelist Billy Graham have been replaced by entertainers, athletes, and popular artists as the individuals whom young people most respect and admire. In surveys taken during each of the past 15 years, for example, General Norman Schwarzkopf was the only world leader chosen as the number-one hero among high school students. Other names on the elite list joined by General Schwarzkopf included Paula Abdul, Michael Jackson, Michael Jordan, Eddie Murphy, Burt Reynolds, and Sylvester Stallone.

More than 30 years have passed since Canadian sociologist Marshall McLuhan first taught us the huge impact that the electronic media has had on how we think, learn, and understand—as well as how we choose our heroes. In the 1960s, Pop artist Andy Warhol predicted that there would soon come a time when every American would be famous for 15 minutes. But if it is easier today to achieve Warhol's 15 minutes of fame, it is also much harder to hold on to it. Reputations are often ruined as quickly as they are made.

And yet, there remain those artists and performers who continue to inspire and instruct us in spite of changes in world events, media technology, or popular tastes. Even in a society as fickle and fast moving as our own, there are still those performers whose work and reputation endure, pop culture legends who inspire an almost religious devotion from their fans.

Why do the works and personalities of some artists continue to fascinate us while others are so quickly forgotten? What, if any, qualities do they share that enable them to have such power over our lives? There are no easy answers to these questions. The artists and entertainers profiled in this series often have little more in common than the enormous influence that each of them has had on our lives.

Some offer us an escape. Artists such as actress Marilyn Monroe, comedian Groucho Marx, and writer Stephen King have used glamour, humor, or fantasy to help us escape from our everyday lives. Others present us with images that are all too recognizable. The uncompromising realism of actor and director Charlie Chaplin and folk singer Bob Dylan challenges us to confront and change the things in our world that most disturb us.

Some offer us friendly, reassuring experiences. The work of animator Walt Disney and late-night talk show host Johnny Carson, for example, provides us with a sense of security and continuity in a changing world. Others shake us up. The best work of composer John Lennon and actor James Dean will always inspire their fans to question and reevaluate the world in which they live.

It is also hard to predict the kind of life that a pop culture legend will lead, or how he or she will react to fame. Popular singers Michael Jackson

and Prince carefully guard their personal lives from public view. Other performers, such as popular singer Madonna, enjoy putting their private lives before the public eye.

What these artists and entertainers do share, however, is the rare ability to capture and hold the public's imagination in a world dominated by mass media and disposable celebrity. In spite of their differences, each of them has somehow managed to achieve legendary status in a popular culture that values novelty and change.

The books in this series examine the lives and careers of these and other pop culture legends, and the society that places such great value on their work. Each book considers the extraordinary talent, the stubborn commitment, and the great personal sacrifice required to create work of enduring quality and influence in today's world.

As you read these books, ask yourself the following questions: How are the careers of these individuals shaped by their society? What role do they play in shaping the world? And what is it that so captivates us about their lives, their work, or the images they present?

Hopefully, by studying the lives and achievements of these pop culture legends, we will learn more about ourselves.

Recognition at Last

I T WAS THE NIGHT that all of Hollywood's rich and powerful dressed in their most expensive, most outrageous, and most elaborate garb. Millions of television viewers watched at home while thousands more lined up along the boulevard with their cameras, waiting to snap pictures of the stars as they arrived at the Dorothy Chandler Pavilion. This was the night that the Hollywood community gathered to honor its own for outstanding achievement in the motion picture industry. The mild Los Angeles evening of March 21, 1994, offered the perfect setting for the annual Academy Awards ceremony, during which the Academy of Motion Picture Arts and Sciences bestows golden Oscar statuettes for distinguished individual or group efforts of the previous year in approximately 25 categories of film acting and production.

As Steven Spielberg walked down the red carpet toward the Dorothy Chandler Pavilion, many television interviewers begged for a moment of his time, for a comment on how he felt about being at the

Spielberg brandishes his twin Oscars—for 1993's Best Director and Best Picture—which he finally won after nearly three decades of blockbuster filmmaking.

awards ceremony with a film that might finally earn him the much-coveted prize for Best Picture. Spielberg introduced his mother, Leah, his wife, Kate Capshaw, and his stepdaughter, Jessica, to the viewing public, a characteristic boyish grin on his face, and offered a few words about his celebrated film—perhaps his masterpiece—*Schindler's List.*

Traditionally the Academy gives the Best Picture award at the very end of the ceremony; all other presentations lead up to the suspenseful moment when the finest film of the year is recognized. Nominees need patience as they clap politely for winners in other categories, and for 46-year-old Steven Spielberg, the wait meant several hours of trying not to bite his nails, a lifelong habit that he has been unable to break. He watched, grinning each time a camera focused on him, as his black-and-white epic about the Holocaust during World War II won several awards.

When his longtime friend and colleague, actor Harrison Ford, announced that Spielberg was the winner of the Best Director award for *Schindler's List,* he was ecstatic. When actor-director Clint Eastwood, who had won both Best Director and Best Picture the previous year for *Unforgiven,* took the stage to present the 1993 winner for Best Picture, the audience once again got ready to applaud the veteran Hollywood director who had brought them such movies as *E. T. The Extra-Terrestrial* and *Jurassic Park.* Eastwood opened the envelope and declared that the Best Picture award for 1993 would go to *Schindler's List.* Although not many in the auditorium, or at home watching on television, were surprised by the announcement, Spielberg himself seemed shocked, thrilled, and overwhelmed.

In his acceptance speech Spielberg urged that awareness about the Holocaust be heightened, that

more courses on the subject be offered in schools, and that people never forget what happened to more than six million Jews and others considered inferior by Adolf Hitler and the Nazis during World War II.

Although it is always exciting to receive the Academy Award for Best Picture, Spielberg believed receiving the prize that night was particularly significant because the Academy had snubbed him several times previously. During his nearly three decades of Hollywood filmmaking, beginning at the age of 20, Spielberg had never won an Academy Award. Many

Oskar Schindler (Liam Neeson) and Itzhak Stern (Ben Kingsley) assemble the list of 1,100 Jews to be protected from the Nazi death camps in *Schindler's List*. Spielberg said this was the first film in which he "told the truth."

people believe that his earlier movies did not deserve the critical recognition of the industry's highest accolade because they were mostly large-scale entertainment extravaganzas, not serious films about life, politics, and art. Others assert that he was deliberately overlooked for various reasons, including jealousy, and because he tried to break out of the mold of movies that he was expected to make.

The other Spielberg film that many people regard as a masterpiece, besides *Schindler's List*, is *E. T. The Extra-Terrestrial*, a movie about a young boy and a small space creature who befriend each other when the alien is trapped on Earth. The movie, which became the number-one box-office hit in America when Universal Studios released it in 1982, was nominated for nine awards but won only three (one for Best Original Score, one for Best Visual Effects, and one for Best Sound Effects Editing), but no prize for Best Picture or Best Director. It was the second time the Best Picture award had eluded Spielberg—the first time was in 1975 for *Jaws*.

The Color Purple, a movie based on Alice Walker's novel of the same name, which Spielberg directed in 1985, received 11 Oscar nominations, but none was for Best Director. It is highly unusual when the Academy nominates a film for Best Picture but does not also acknowledge the director with a Best Director nomination. Warner Bros., the studio that released the film, placed an ad in Hollywood trade papers announcing that it was shocked and angry that *The Color Purple's* primary creative force, Spielberg, was not nominated for the award and thus was not recognized for his work.

Spielberg's intent when he made *Schindler's List* was not to win an Academy Award, but the award brought recognition to the film and highlighted its importance. He told a reporter for *USA Today* in December 1993, "[I]f the only thing that comes out of *Schindler's List* is that there are more Holocaust study courses in high schools across the country, we will have accomplished a great deal." He added, "I've often wondered why Jewish leaders during the golden era of motion picture production didn't celebrate their own heritage by bringing Jewish stories to the screen. It's probably because in those days, immigrant Jewish producers were having an identity struggle just wanting to become Americans."

Spielberg made the picture because he believed he had to, compelled by his desire not only to come to terms with his own identity as a Jew but also to direct films that deal with serious human and political issues. In 1982, the film critic Andrew Sarris had written about Spielberg's weakness in depicting mature human relationships in his films: "There is still too much of the world between the children's room and outer space left unexplored in the cinema of Steven Spielberg. He does not have to remake *The Grapes of Wrath* [director John Ford's classic 1940 movie recounting the story of depression-era farmers in the dust bowl]. All I ask is that sometime before he reaches the age of fifty, he should become somewhat more skeptical of his own self-induced euphoria."

Spielberg believes that he could not have made his epic film *Schindler's List* any earlier in his career: "It took me years before I was really ready to make *Schindler's List*." Many of Spielberg's friends maintain that *Schindler's List* has transformed the director, marking the continuation of a self-reflective process that began shortly after the birth of his first child, Max, in 1985. Spielberg has generally been known as a director who works very well with children and who perhaps never really wanted to grow up himself, but *Schindler's List* bears witness that the genius boy–wonder director, who took Hollywood by storm in his mid–20s, had decided to become an adult.

There are many reasons why Spielberg chose to make movies about children and creatures from outer space, to deal with childhood fears and fantastical stories. Some reasons directly relate to his own childhood and the impressions it left on him. Another explanation is that he started making movies right after adolescence and had not really matured enough to deal with serious, adult situations. But, whether the stories in his films were serious or whimsical, there was never any doubt that Spielberg knew how to handle moviemaking.

Actor Dennis Weaver met the 23-year-old Spielberg in 1971 when he was cast in the young director's first made–for–TV movie, *Duel.* "I had never worked with more than two cameras on a film," Weaver recalled, "and we went out to shoot the final scene where the truck goes over the cliff and Steven had five cameras out there to shoot that one scene. I thought 'Boy, this young fellow really has moxie.'" Spielberg went on from television movies to full-length features, eventually leading up to his first big-screen hit, *Jaws.*

Although with *Schindler's List* Spielberg has made the quintessential "grown–up" film, it is doubtful whether he will retire all the creatures and monsters that have inhabited most of his previous work. The same year that *Schindler's List* was released, *Jurassic Park*, Spielberg's horror/science-fiction/adventure movie about dinosaurs coming back to life, made box–office history. Although *E.T.* holds the American record to date ($399.8 million), *Jurassic Park* stands as the highest-grossing movie worldwide ($900 million).

With *Close Encounters of the Third Kind* and *E.T.,*

Spielberg explored his interest in creatures from other planets, and with *Jurassic Park* he indulged in another childhood fascination. Dinosaurs were the stars of the movie thanks in part to Spielberg's generous use of the latest computer technology. Most of Spielberg's films have taken advantage of cutting-edge technology to deliver fantastic special effects and fast-paced action sequences, as in his films *Raiders of the Lost Ark, Indiana Jones and the Temple of Doom*, and *Indiana Jones and the Last Crusade.*

Spielberg has established a reputation for being enamored of technical wizardry. At his production

Longtime friend and colleague Harrison Ford congratulates an ecstatic Spielberg for winning his two Oscars.

Spielberg receives a kiss from his wife, Kate Capshaw, as he celebrates his triumph with his mother, Leah Adler.

company, Amblin, he and his staff play video games on a daily basis. At home Spielberg indulges in computer games with friends who live in other cities, via modems. In 1994 he spent time at the Consumer Electronics Show in Las Vegas, Nevada, investigating the latest in technological gadgetry. There he saw the impact his movies had had on the computer industry, with games, programs, videos, and other products based on *Jurassic Park, Raiders of the Lost Ark, Close Encounters of the Third Kind,* and *Jaws.* Moreover, in the late 1990s he is exploring uncharted territory as the head of a studio. In August 1994 Spielberg, Jeffrey Katzenberg, a former top executive at Walt Disney Company, and David Geffen, a self-made billionaire in the entertainment industry, announced plans to open the first major new Hollywood studio in 60 years.

Throughout his career Spielberg has tried new approaches to filmmaking while conveying his unique vision of the world. In the *New Yorker* magazine on March 21, 1994, one critic wrote, "The way Steven Spielberg sees the world has become the way the world is communicated back to us." Many critics claim that one can spot a Spielberg project even before reading the opening credits; in reality, Spielberg has been constantly reinventing himself with each movie he has made.

Winning the Academy Awards' highest prize for *Schindler's List*, which many critics believe has already become one of the most poignant films of all time, was significant for Spielberg, but it does not mean he is finished searching for other profound and important projects. Although he has made a serious film and will probably make others, he hopes never to lose that ability to please the child in each moviegoer that has delighted so many over the years. As he once said, "I'm growing up, but I think I am simply becoming an older Peter Pan. The one thing I don't want to lose is the fairy dust. I don't think any filmmaker can afford to lose that kind of magic."

2 Childhood Impressions

WHEN WORLD WAR II ENDED in 1945, the United States entered an era of postwar optimism and opportunity. Most people believed that every American family, through hard work and thrift, could have a house in the suburbs, two cars in the garage, a refrigerator, and a television set. Television was poised to revolutionize the entertainment industry by bringing visual entertainment (as compared to radio bringing only sound) into more homes than ever before. Steven Spielberg was born into this prosperous and dynamic time on December 18, 1947, in Cincinnati, Ohio.

Soon after Steven's birth, his parents, Arnold and Leah (Posner) Spielberg, moved the family from Cincinnati to Haddonfield, New Jersey. The family was a peripatetic one because Arnold's job in the budding computer industry required him to relocate often. An electrical engineer, Arnold was very interested in technology and the emerg-

Although considered tame viewing, Disney films such as *Snow White*, with its intense and vivid images, both frightened and stimulated the imagination of the young Spielberg.

ing field of computers, and he believed that people would greatly benefit from this new invention. In fact, Arnold Spielberg was part of a team of scientists who designed some of the first computers. The elder Spielberg introduced his son to technology at an early age, and this technical knowledge would greatly influence Steven when he began to make films.

Leah Spielberg's interests were very different from her husband's. She was a classical pianist, played in a small chamber orchestra, and was involved in cultural and artistic pursuits. Growing up, as Spielberg once said, in "a house with three screaming younger sisters and a mother who played concert piano with seven other women" probably contributed to Steven's belief that he was raised almost exclusively in a world of women. Although his sisters, Anne, Nancy, and Sue, were a formidable feminine trio in his childhood, they also came in handy when Steven needed actors for his early films.

Arnold bought the family's first movie camera, an eight-millimeter home model, when Steven was four years old, and the young boy showed an immediate interest in the machine. Not long after, Arnold took his young son to see his first motion picture, Cecil B. DeMille's 1952 cinematic extravaganza *The Greatest Show on Earth*, a drama about the circus world. Steven's father told him that the movie would be bigger than he was, that people would be up on the screen, but that they could not get off the screen and hurt him. Nevertheless, young Steven was overwhelmed by the experience and, as many children do, he thought the characters and situations in the movie were real. The scene he remembered most clearly from the movie was the action-packed train wreck sequence when the lions and other circus animals escape from their cages. To Steven, who had a big imagination, the train appeared to leap off the screen and land in his lap. The movie made a lasting impression on him.

During Steven's childhood, Walt Disney's films were very popular because they were considered to be family entertainment and suitable for viewing by children. They were not particularly violent, they did not deal with adult issues, and they told wholesome stories. But for many children Disney's movies held moments of terror. Steven himself was alarmed by *Snow White* and *Fantasia*. After seeing *Bambi*, he told his parents he was frightened by the fire in the story. The vibrant and fantastical fairy tales brought to life onscreen in these films probably increased the scope of Steven's already active imagination.

As a child, Steven spent a lot of time watching television, but his parents were very careful about not letting him watch too much TV in general, and disturbing shows in particular. To make sure that he did not spend all his time in front of the television, they draped a blanket over the set. Nonetheless, the shows and movies Steven did watch, such as Frank Capra's *It's a Wonderful Life* and the films of John Ford, Alfred Hitchcock, and Preston Sturges, played a big role in his early ideas for his own movies. Television helped young Steven realize that it was possible to bring the stories in his mind to life. Because Steven was always telling his father how to shoot family movies, Arnold soon gave his son the camera to record familial events. Steven began using the movie camera to record his family's camping trips as well as daily life in his home.

Leah Speilberg recounted that she was never able to decorate her house completely because her son needed space for his productions: "I lived in a beautiful house and I got as far as the carpeting, drapes and a Steinway [piano] and then he took over, and my

The train wreck scene in *The Greatest Show on Earth* had a nearly physical impact upon the young Spielberg, who believed he saw the train literally leap off the screen. Soon he would stage and film miniature train wrecks with his own model locomotive set and the family's eight-millimeter camera.

house from the time I can remember it was a studio." One day the young director even talked his mother into letting a pot of Cherries Jubilee boil over onto the stove just so he could film the bubbly, gooey fruit. Apparently, when she asked her son to film the family

24

in their car, he decided that the hubcaps were far more interesting and shot them instead.

Although Steven's overactive imagination often transformed harmless objects in his bedroom at night into frightening monsters and creatures, he was not

Disney's *Bambi* distressed Spielberg, whose young but volatile imagination was easily inflamed.

innocent of playing scary pranks on his younger sisters. One night, when his mother and father returned from an evening out, they found Steven in home-made monster makeup, created from wet green toilet paper. His sisters were found, terrified, in their rooms.

While Steven fantasized about monsters and aliens, he was actually part of a relatively normal, middle-class, suburban household where the father earned a living to support the family and the mother raised the children. Even though his family moved a number of times and his parents frequently argued, he grew up in a world where his mother always prepared the meals and his father went to work each day. It is this traditional setting that is so often featured as the backdrop for extraordinary events in Steven's movies. His mother once said that when people watch *E.T.*, they "are viewing our family at the dinner table."

26

★ CHILDHOOD IMPRESSIONS ★

When Steven was nine, his family moved from New Jersey to the sunny desert setting of Scottsdale, Arizona, a suburb of Phoenix. Many believe that the years he spent in Scottsdale, from ages 9 to 17, left some of the most lasting impressions on him. The asphalt-lined streets and driveways and the neighborhoods of houses built closely together look strikingly similar to the communities Spielberg would later include in his films *Poltergeist* and *E.T.* Steven felt bored in the dull, quiet suburban world of his childhood and made movies to fight this boredom. He soon discovered, he later said, that he "could do anything or live anywhere via [his] imagination, through film."

His room, which he shared with many animals and birds, including free-flying parakeets, was always the safest and most comforting place for him. There he could escape from his feelings of loneliness, from monotony, from the hostility of schoolmates (he was reclusive, scrawny, unathletic, and not very motivated at school), and from the disapproving eye of his father. His interest in space, stars, and extraterrestrial life began when he was six and his father woke him up one night to witness a meteor storm in a nearby field. His father tried to explain the technical aspects of what was happening, but all Steven could do was watch in amazement at what he imagined were falling stars. A few decades later this scene from his child-hood appeared in the movie *Close Encounters of the Third Kind* almost exactly as Steven remembered it.

In his room he created imaginary playmates, including one special character from outer space. Steven enjoyed the company of his imaginary friends because they never left him. In his real life, by the time Steven made friends in one place, his father's job would require the family to leave, and the young boy would have to start all over again. "At the moment of

27

my greatest comfort and tranquillity," Steven says, "we'd move somewhere else. . . . And the older I got, the harder it got." One story in particular conveys the feelings Spielberg had of being an outcast and being unacceptable by his peers:

> The height of my wimpery came when we had to run a mile for a grade in elementary school. The whole class of fifty finished, except for two people left on the track[,] me and a mentally retarded boy. Of course, *he* ran awkwardly, but I was just never able to run. I was maybe forty yards ahead of him, and I was only 100 yards away from the finish line. The whole class turned and began rooting for the young retarded boy—cheering him on, saying, "C'mon, c'mon, beat Spielberg! Run, run!" It was like he came to life for the first time, and he began to pour it on but still not fast enough to beat me. And I remember thinking, "Okay, now how am I gonna fall and make it look like I really fell?" And I remember actually stepping on my toe and going face hard into the red clay of the track and actually scraping my nose. Everybody cheered when I fell, and then they began to really scream for this guy: "C'mon John, c'mon, run, run!" I got up just as John came up behind me, and I began running as if to beat him, but not really to win, running to *let him* win. We were nose to nose, and suddenly I laid back a step, then a half-step. Suddenly he was ahead . . . and then he crossed the finish line ahead of me. Everybody grabbed this guy, and they threw him up on their shoulders and carried him into the locker room, into the showers, and I stood there on the track field and cried my eyes out for five minutes. I'd never felt better and I'd never felt worse in my entire life.

Although Steven perceived himself as not having many friends during his childhood and adolescence, not everyone in his family remembers this as being so. His sister Anne, who is two years younger, recalled, "He had more friends than he remembers having. . . . If you looked at a picture of him then, you'd say, 'Yes, there's a nerd.' There's the crewcut, the flattop, there are the ears. There's the skinny body. But he really had an incredible personality. He could make everything he was going to do sound like you wished you were a part of it."

Feeling different and apart from the crowd gave Steven plenty of time to create imaginary characters and situations, which he would later turn into amateur and then professional films. He claims that by the age of 12 or 13 he knew he wanted to be a filmmaker. One way Steven engaged his peers was to cast them in his movies, which made it possible for him to get along with other children without sacrificing his artistic bent.

One particular neighborhood bully would frequently knock Steven down or hold his face in the water fountain. After one too many afternoons of running home scared, Steven offered the bully the starring role in a war movie called *Battle Squad*. The bully was cast as the squad leader, and from that point on the two boys were friends. Being picked on by a bully left an indelible impression on the young Steven. Years later, when he was working on the script for the movie *Back to the Future*, he included a gang of tough youths who constantly harass the main character.

Steven would spend many hours in his room staging train wrecks with his model locomotive set and inventing simple but convincing special effects. He filmed his creations from many different angles and positions, working to get the impression he was after. He would often be eye-level with the tracks to see what the train was going to look like when it crashed. This attention to camera angles, to see what the camera saw, would become a trademark of his future filming technique. When he was 12, Steven bought his own movie camera, and he was rarely seen without it.

The following year, at age 13, Steven enrolled in a Boy Scout photography class. During the class he made a three-minute film about a cowboy who robs a stagecoach, in which he cast a friend as the cowboy. The film impressed his Boy Scout troop leaders, and they awarded him the first of many prizes for his film-making—a merit badge and a promotion to Eagle Scout, the next level in the Scouts. The success of his first movie project inspired Steven, and he began working on other ideas for films.

At home everything became worth shooting, even the most routine tasks, such as his mother opening a can of beans or his father cleaning a fish. His interest in shooting film overpowered everything else in his life, and his schoolwork suffered. Steven was not interested in what his teachers had to say and could not see how subjects like math, science, and languages would help him make better movies. Author D. L. Maybery notes in his biography of Steven Spielberg, "Instead of studying in class, Steven made little draw-ings in the margins of his textbooks. On page after page he would draw little figures, so when he flipped through the book, the images would move like a car-toon."

His first fully scripted film was a 40-minute war story entitled *Escape to Nowhere*, which he made in 1961 when he was nearly 14. In high school Steven had no less than 15 short films to his credit, and a local newspaper, the *Phoenix Gazette*, published a story about the aspiring filmmaker. To raise money for his productions, Steven whitewashed citrus trees (to help keep snakes and rodents from eating the fruit) in his neighborhood during his spare time. Another way he

Disney's *Fantasia*, too, offered plenty of material for the nightmares of an over-imaginative child.

acquired funds was by turning the living room into a miniature movie theater. He rented films, had his mother and sisters make popcorn, and charged admission. The first attempt brought him $36, which he promptly donated to the local school for children with disabilities instead of using to make a movie.

Although incidents at school—like being teased for vomiting while trying to dissect a frog in biology class—continued to be painful to him, Steven was soon enrolled in a program where his artistic inclinations were not only tolerated but encouraged. It was in the theater and arts program at Phoenix's Arcadia High School that he finally met other students with similar interests in the performing arts. He met youngsters who liked acting and drama, and he realized that the world was not divided between jocks and wimps. Furthermore, Steven had to resolve for himself whether he would pursue an artistic career or a scientific one, having to choose between his mother's passion and his father's. Throughout his filmmaking career, he has managed to combine both.

The theater and arts program gave Steven the confidence and encouragement he needed to continue his filmmaking, and at the age of 16 he made his first full-length film. The movie was a science-fiction story about a group of scientists investigating mysterious lights in the night sky. He called the two-and-a-half-hour movie *Firelight* and cast his entire family in the picture. The movie was longer than most films shown in theaters and cost Steven $500 to make. He was responsible for the entire production, from writing the story to casting the actors, and was in charge from start to finish.

Firelight took Steven a year to shoot because he had to work on the film mostly on the weekends. He missed many days of school by feigning illness, holding a thermometer to a lightbulb to make it appear as though he had a fever. His mother became aware of this trick but realized how important the film was to her son and let him stay home. After all, Leah was herself an artist and identified with Steven's passionate desire to work on his creation.

However, when he nearly failed in school, Steven's parents threatened to take away his equipment unless he did some schoolwork. It became clear that Steven's father wanted his son eventually to work in a scientific field rather than focusing so intently on moviemaking. Steven recalled, "My father had a map he tried to get me to follow. He wanted me to be an electrical engineer or a doctor so he was very strict with me regarding all the high school courses that would lead me in those directions, such as maths or chemistry, which I was intuitively horrible at. Of course I took the opposite trail and followed my mother's footsteps." By taking the "opposite trail," Steven became more and more distant from his father as Arnold himself grew more estranged from his wife and family.

Steven's family problems compelled him to focus on his filmmaking—his escape—even more intently. "I was surrounded by so much negativity when I was a kid," he later explained, "that I had no recourse but to be positive." When he completed *Firelight*, he convinced a Phoenix movie theater manager to show the film for one night. He was able to sell enough tickets to recover the cost of making the movie and even earned a profit of $100.

Soon after *Firelight's* premiere, the Spielbergs moved from a suburb of Phoenix to Saratoga, near San Jose, California, in 1963. Sixteen-year-old Steven was once again faced with attending a new school and making another set of friends. Adding to these pressures was his parents' separation and then their divorce in 1965. Steven noted that his parents' marriage was never really a cheerful one and that they probably stayed together as long as they did to protect their four children from unhappiness. But the children knew their parents did not get along. Steven recalled, "My sisters and I would stay up at night, listening to our parents argue."

Although his mother and father's divorce greatly affected and saddened Steven, it did not stop him from pursuing his dream of making movies. A fateful trip to Universal Studios in 1965 launched Steven on his way to becoming one of the most remarkable filmmakers in history.

Breaking into the Business

3

DURING THE 1960s the United States experienced tumultuous social upheaval, with many young people questioning governmental, religious, and parental authority. These rebellious young adults, who dressed unconventionally, grew their hair long, and turned their backs on the materialistic world of their parents, tried to find their own answers to problems. It was a time of "free love," when young men and women lived openly with one another without marriage, and a time of experimentation with mind-altering psychedelic drugs, which produced hallucinogenic effects, and marijuana. It was also the decade of the "British invasion," as bands such as the Beatles, the Rolling Stones, and the Dave Clark 5 transformed America's popular music. But the era was also marked by the assassination of President John F. Kennedy in 1963 and America's controversial involvement in the Vietnam War, which embroiled the country from the mid-1950s to the war's end in 1975. In 1968 Americans were further shocked by the murders of civil rights leader Martin Luther King, Jr., and President Kennedy's brother, Senator Robert F. Kennedy. In the midst of all this cultural and politi-

Universal Studios in 1965, when Spielberg—17 years old and brashly determined—tricked his way in for a free summer apprenticeship.

cal change, Spielberg attended high school in California, graduated, and then began to pursue a career in filmmaking.

Spielberg's first years in California as a high school student were difficult, and he turned away from school and his crumbling family life and focused almost exclusively on making movies. He graduated from Saratoga High School in the spring of 1965. That summer, his preoccupation with film brought him to Hollywood's Universal Studios, a motion picture production facility, which he visited as part of a tour group. While touring the studio, the 17-year-old movie buff soon became bored and restless because the guide did not show the group actual movies in progress. Spielberg wanted to see the soundstages where films were being shot, not the usual tourist attractions, such as the cafeteria and old sets. According to Spielberg biographer Philip Taylor, Spielberg sneaked away from the group during a bathroom break and made his way to a soundstage. While wandering around the soundstage by himself, Spielberg met by chance Chuck Silvers, head of Universal's editorial department. Spielberg later recalled, "Instead of calling the guards to throw me off the lot, he talked to me for about an hour.... He said he'd like to see some of my little films, and so he gave me a pass to get on the lot the next day." When Spielberg showed up with films in hand the following day, Silvers said he enjoyed watching the movies, and complimented the young director on his work. Silvers could only offer Spielberg verbal encouragement; he was unable to do anything more for the aspiring filmmaker.

Spielberg, however, was not discouraged by Silvers's inability to help him, and the next day he made a bold move to get himself inside the doors of the studio without a pass. Dressed in a business suit and carrying one of his father's old briefcases, Spielberg walked straight through the front gate, waved to the guard (who thought he was the son of MCA-Universal's head, Lew Wasserman), and walked right into the studio. "So every day that summer," remembered Spielberg, "I went in my suit and hung out with directors and writers and editors and dubbers. I found an office that wasn't being used and became a squatter. I went to a camera store, bought some plastic name titles and put my name in the building directory. Steven Spielberg, Room 22C."

Even though he now had access to many employees and a few movie executives, he could not get anyone but Silvers to look at his films. One reason for this might have been the type of film, 8-millimeter, on which his movies were shot—most commercial motion pictures were either shot on 16-millimeter or 35-millimeter film.

Inevitably the summer came to an end, and it was time for Spielberg to return to school. Much to his and his parents' relief, Spielberg headed to California State University at Long Beach that fall. He had wanted to study film in an academic environment, but his high school grades were below average and he was not admitted to any of the major film programs, such as those at the University of California at Los Angeles (UCLA) or the University of Southern California (USC).

Although the university at Long Beach did not offer a formal film program, it accepted Spielberg into the English program, which he chose in part because he believed his knowledge of literature was lacking. While Spielberg attended school on the two days that he had scheduled classes, he spent the rest of his time in cinemas watching movies. He also spent a lot of time at Universal Studios observing filmmakers ply their trade and was told one day that if he made movies on 16-millimeter film, top studio executives might actually look at them. On one occasion he was able to sneak onto the soundstage of an Alfred Hitchcock film, *Torn Curtain*, before an assistant director threw him off the set.

Spielberg worked part-time jobs to raise money for a film he was writing and convinced a wealthy college friend, Dennis Hoffman, to help finance the film. Hoffman, who wanted to be a movie producer, gave Spielberg $10,000 on the condition that he would become the film's producer, responsible for raising and organizing the money for a movie in order to pay the actors and to buy film, equipment, set material, and props. While Spielberg diligently labored on the project that he believed would offer him entree into Universal Studios, his coursework suffered.

The final product of all his labor and planning was a 22-minute film entitled *Amblin'* (short for "rambling"; also the name of the production company Spielberg established in 1984). A silent film about a girl and a boy who hitchhike from the Mojave Desert to the Pacific Ocean, it took Spielberg 10 days to shoot. Whereas movies often take only a few weeks or months to shoot, the preproduction (raising money, scouting locations, and finding actors) and postproduction work (editing and reshooting scenes) can add many more months to the project. Although today Spielberg dismisses the film as a "slick by-product of a kid immersed up to his nose in film," *Amblin'* was the first of the 20-year-old director's short films to get him noticed at Universal. He adds, "*Amblin'* was a conscious effort to break into the business and become successful by proving to people I could move a camera and compose nicely and deal with lighting and performances."

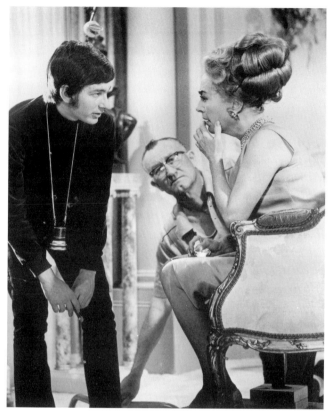

Spielberg's first television program was an episode of Rod Serling's *Night Gallery* starring Joan Crawford. The legendary actress later proclaimed Spielberg a genius.

When Spielberg approached Universal with *Amblin'*, he came to them with an impressive knowledge of the films he had spent the previous years watching and studying. He was greatly influenced by many distinguished directors, including John Ford, Preston Sturges, and Frank Capra. Both Ford and Capra focused on telling dramatic stories in epic moviemaking style, where simple, everyday people are pitted against overwhelming circumstances. In most of their films, good ultimately triumphs over evil, a theme for which Spielberg's films would also be noted.

As Spielberg watched other directors' films, he observed camera angles, how actors moved from one scene to the next, and how a story was told with visual images. By analyzing film after film, he was slowly developing his own ideas about how to make movies.

His friend at Universal, Chuck Silvers, showed *Amblin'* to a number of top executives, including Sidney J. Sheinberg, head of Universal's television production. Sheinberg immediately offered Spielberg a seven-year contract to direct television programs for the studio, saying, "Sir, I liked your work. How would you like to go to work professionally?" Spielberg left college so quickly that he did not even have time to clean out his locker. Although he feared his father would be angry, Spielberg believed he was making the right decision for himself. Many other directors, such as Robert Altman and Arthur Penn, never finished college. Spielberg was even more confident that he had made the right decision when *Amblin'* won the Atlanta Film Festival award and an award at a festival in Venice, Italy, in 1969. His 22-minute film was also nationally distributed in 1970 with the Paramount film *Love Story*, which became a box-office hit and was nominated for several Academy Awards.

Although Spielberg would later regret signing a contract that bound him to television for seven years, he reported to work on the first day with great enthusiasm. His initial directing assignment was an episode of Rod Serling's *Night Gallery*, about a blind woman who blackmails her doctor into performing an operation that will allow her to see her cherished New York City again, only to be confronted by the city's notorious 1965 power blackout. The segment was to star legendary film actress Joan Crawford and to air on November 8, 1969.

In this episode, called "Eyes," Spielberg used several techniques and formulas that he had learned from other films. Because he was searching for a style that would distinguish the episode, he employed techniques that were used in many European art films from the 1950s and 1960s, particularly those favored by a group of filmmakers in the French New Wave movement. The New Wave (*Nouvelle Vague*) filmmakers turned out their first feature films between 1958 and 1960. Leading members included Francois Truffaut, Jean-Luc Godard, and Louis Malle, who rejected conventional forms of filmmaking and endorsed a freer style, often dealing candidly with sex and using symbolism to articulate plot. Along the same lines, Spielberg, in this episode about a rich blind woman, shot many scenes involving mirrors and reflections to symbolize the vision she so desperately desires. When the shooting was completed, Joan Crawford declared the 22-year-old director a genius. He had directed the esteemed Hollywood star as if he were a veteran of many projects, not someone who had embarked on his first professional job.

The episode impressed many of the studio executives, and Spielberg went on to direct several other programs for the NBC network at Universal Studios. His projects included episodes of shows that were very popular in the late 1960s and early 1970s: *Marcus Welby, M.D.*, *The Name of the Game*, *Owen Marshall*, *The Psychiatrists*, and *Columbo*. Spielberg considers two episodes of *The Psychiatrists* from 1971 to be his best television work. One, "The Private World of Martin Dalton," is about a six-year-old boy who is lost in a fantasy world and is analyzed by the title character. The other, "Par for the Course," is about a golf pro who learns he is dying of cancer and turns to the title character to help him cope. At the end of the episode, two of the pro's friends present him with the 18th hole from a golf course in a shoe box. Spielberg explained, "He tore the grass out of the hole and he squeezed the dirt all over himself and he thanked them for bringing this gift, the greatest gift he ever received. It was just a very moving moment."

After Spielberg directed several impressive television programs, the studio offered him the opportunity to direct films for TV. He had experimented with styles and techniques while directing programs, each time developing and honing his skills, and he felt confident he could tackle movies. During the early 1970s, he directed three films for Universal; the first, and most successful, was *Duel*.

In *Duel*, Dennis Weaver, who was well known for his roles in such television series as *McCloud*, *Gunsmoke*, and *Kentucky Jones*, starred as ordinary traveling salesman David Mann, who is stalked by the driver of an ominous black truck. The 73-minute film was first telecast by ABC on November 13, 1971, and was so popular on American television that Universal Studios decided to release it in European theaters, where it became a big hit. Spielberg has always

Having proved himself as a director of television programs, Spielberg moved to television films. In his first, *Duel* (starring Dennis Weaver), about a traveling salesman stalked by a black truck, he created and sustained the tension with his expressive use of sound and his effective decision never to show the truck driver.

enjoyed great success in Europe, where his polished visual images and tension-building stories have attracted large audiences. Part of *Duel's* great appeal is the uneasiness it creates by never showing the truck driver or explaining the anonymous villain's motives. All through the movie, David Mann tries to escape his pursuer, only to be terrorized at every turn. At the end, the hero dances as he watches the metallic menace drive off a cliff and become engulfed in flames.

Reviewer Janet Maslin of the *New York Times* wrote, "*Duel* looks like the work of an unusually talented young director . . . it might almost have been a silent film, because it expresses so much through action and so little through words." Douglas Brode, who wrote *The Films of Steven Spielberg* (1995), believes, however, that *Duel* is totally dependent on sound:

> The contrasting engines of the sad, small car and the huge, threatening truck, as well as the striking authentic, highly expressive noises heard in each of the hamlets both drivers pass through, are effectively blended with the evocative music. The film's edge-of-your-seat suspense derives as much from its sounds as its sights, which would likewise be true of the director's future films.

In February 1973 the film won the Grand Prix de Festival award in Avoriaz, France, and Spielberg received the Cariddi D'Oro for his direction at the Taormina Film Festival in Rome, Italy, in mid-July. It was the first time a made-for-TV movie had been so honored. With *Duel* a smash in Europe, Spielberg was even more anxious to make a movie for American theaters. He was, however, still committed to his seven-year contract with Universal Television.

During a lull in television projects at Universal, Spielberg started several small productions that he hoped would offer him access into feature filmmaking. One project was *Ace Eli and Rodger of the Skies*, which Spielberg had written and submitted to producers David Brown and Richard Zanuck. Although Spielberg wanted to direct, the producers decided he was not quite ready and decided to buy the script from him instead. Twentieth Century-Fox assigned an established scriptwriter and another director to the film, which was about the barnstorming of a World War I aviator and his son. A couple of years later Brown and Zanuck would work with the head of Universal Studios, Lew Wasserman, and would be given the chance to move Universal back into the field of theatrical moviemaking. Spielberg would be reintroduced to the pair of producers when they joined Universal, and the two would give him his first feature film opportunity.

Before shooting his first feature, however, Spielberg made the next two movies in his television trilogy. The films, both made in 1972, were fairly straightforward in plot and theme: *Something Evil* is the story of a family who buys a farm with a curse on it. The family fights against the demon in their new home and triumphs. *Savage*, which was apparently the pilot for a TV series that never made it into production, involves a Supreme Court nominee who is being blackmailed and two journalists who try to uncover the mystery. In both films Spielberg worked with renowned actors, including Sandy Dennis, Darren McGavin, Ralph Bellamy, Barry Sullivan, Barbara Bain, and Martin Landau, and exhibited the same professional control and knowledge that he had in previous projects.

One reason Spielberg's three television films turned out to be so visually appealing and dramatically tense was that he used storyboards extensively. Spielberg has always been admired for his storyboards—hand-drawn cards that break down the shooting of a film into detailed pictures (describing camera angles, direction, and actors' movements) that represent how the scenes should look once they are shot on film. According to Brode, Spielberg systematically blocked out the whole film *Duel* in this picture-book form on IBM cards, each card holding the main point of the scene, the angle Spielberg would take on it, and how many camera setups he required. Consequently, essential alterations and edits are done to scenes in the movie before the camera ever rolls.

When he had completed his television trilogy in 1973, Spielberg was relieved of his contractual obligations, and his career as a television director came to an end. Not long after, Brown and Zanuck offered Spielberg his first feature film, entitled *White Lightning*, starring Burt Reynolds. Spielberg had a script of his own that he wanted produced, but he could not muster interest in the project. He worked on *White Lightning* for three months but dropped out when he realized the movie was not what he wanted to do for his first feature. Set in the South, the melodrama is about a convict (played by Reynolds) who escapes to avenge the murder of his brother by a corrupt sheriff. Joseph Sargent replaced Spielberg as director of the film, and Spielberg said later, "I didn't want to start my career as a hard hat journeyman director. I wanted to do something a little more personal."

Thanks to his tenacity, Spielberg soon got the go-ahead on his own project, a fact-based movie he had submitted to Universal years before, and *The Sugarland Express* was off and running.

4 Success Comes Early

NOTING THE SUCCESS of Spielberg's *Duel*, both on American television and in European theaters, Richard Zanuck and David Brown, who had joined Universal, gave the up-and-coming filmmaker his first chance at directing a project that he had also written, *The Sugarland Express*.

Lew Wasserman had some reservations about the money-making potential of the film but decided that because the budget for the picture was so small, he would not stop the producers from going ahead with the project. He told them, "Make the film, fellows. . . . But you may not be playing to full theaters."

The idea for the movie came from a news story that Spielberg had seen in the Los Angeles *Citizen News*. The article told of a Texas couple who hijacked a police car, with the policeman still inside the vehi-

---

Spielberg directs William Atherton and Goldie Hawn in *The Sugarland Express*, his first feature film, which was inspired by a newspaper story about a Texas couple who hijacked a police car (and officer) to help them rescue their baby from a foster home.

cle, and forced the policeman to drive them to a foster home in Sugarland, Texas, where they planned to rescue their baby. Spielberg wrote the original story for the movie but worked on the script with two members of the USC graduating class of 1967, Hal Barwood and Matthew Robbins. Other members of the class, including George Lucas (who later became celebrated for directing *Star Wars*), would become his close collaborators on other projects for years to come. Although a new breed of filmmakers (Martin Scorsese, Francis Ford Coppola, Brian De Palma) was making its way into the movie world and avoiding the control of studios by starting their own production companies, when Spielberg began *The Sugarland Express*, he was still tied to a studio whose executives made the ultimate decisions concerning his first feature.

The Sugarland Express is the story of petty criminals Lou Jean Poplin (played by Goldie Hawn) and Clovis Poplin (William Atherton) and their rip-roaring road trip through Texas in a police car to liberate their son from a foster home. Since Lou Jean had been put in jail for minor crimes, and Clovis was already in prison, the authorities have declared the Poplins unfit parents. Lou Jean needs her husband's help to get their son back, so she is determined to help him escape from prison. Once they are on their way, the media hears of their story, and a publicity convoy begins to follow the couple on their journey. Dysfunctional families, motherhood, and ordinary people placed in extraordinary circumstances in which they must fight overwhelming odds to survive are recurring themes here and in Spielberg's later films.

Spielberg shot his first feature on a new type of camera offered by Panavision, a prominent movie

camera manufacturer. He was the first director select-
ed by Panavision to test the newly developed Panaflex
35-millimeter camera on film. (The Panaflex, which
was noiseless, had a rotating mirror shutter and an
interchangeable lens; it was the first 35-millimeter
camera that could be hand-held and had crystal sync
motors that allowed for more accurate film-to-sound
matching.) A trademark of Spielberg's films has been
the use of cutting-edge computer and filmmaking
technology to further the storytelling aspects of his
movies.

The Sugarland Express, as Lew Wasserman predicted, was only a moderate financial success, but many
critics gave the film glowing reviews, complimenting
Spielberg on his expert technique with the camera.
They were quick to note in one shot the intricate
maneuvers of many vehicles snaking their way across
the parched Texas landscape. Reviewer Paul D.
Zimmerman wrote in Newsweek, "In this world the
cars are like four-wheeled robots. . . . They hunt in
packs and caravans, greedily sucking gas stations
dry. . . . Sometimes they crash into each other in acts
of spectacular stupidity . . . [and] trail the trio with a
prudence that borders on cowardice." Zimmerman
and other critics pointed out that the cars, in many
respects, were more spectacular than the people.
Throughout Spielberg's career, film critics have
remarked that technological brilliance and fantastic
effects often overshadow the human characters in
many of his movies.

In The Sugarland Express, Spielberg pays homage
to one of his favorite childhood cartoons, the Road
Runner series. In one scene, Lou Jean and Clovis
watch Wile E. Coyote and Road Runner enact their
chase sequence on a drive-in theater screen. Spielberg
clearly wants his audience to understand the joke he is

making—that his characters are similar to the characters in the cartoon. However, "if . . . he had liked Lou Jean and Clovis as well," wrote Donald R. Mott and Cheryl McAllister Saunders in their book *Twayne's Filmmakers Series: Steven Spielberg* (1986), "*Sugarland Express* would have been a better film." Spotlighting the Road Runner cartoons would not be the only instance of Spielberg projecting an image, negative or positive, from his own childhood experiences onto the movie screen.

Whatever the shortcomings of *The Sugarland Express*, nearly everyone agreed that a new film talent had emerged from the directorial ranks of Universal Television. The film ultimately made a small profit after it was sold to television, but at the box office it did not make much of a splash. One reason may have been its competition. At almost the same time that *The Sugarland Express* was released in 1974, two other studios (Warner Bros. and United Artists) presented films with plots about young killer-crooks, Terrence Malick's *Badlands* and Robert Altman's *Thieves Like Us*. All the films suffered financially because moviegoers were reluctant to spend money to see three movies that appeared to have such similar plots.

Spielberg believed his movie suffered because of the way he had structured it, trying to weave three different storylines together at the same time (Lou Jean and Clovis on the run; Captain Tanner, chief highway patrolman, following them; and the media in hot pursuit). Mott and Saunders, who wrote a book on Spielberg in 1986, believe that the filmmaker attempted to balance parallel actions in the story but that he is "at his best with a linear storyline and one or two central characters." Despite Spielberg's ambivalence about *The Sugarland Express*, the film won the Best

Peter Benchley's novel *Jaws* so terrified Spielberg that he said he wanted to direct a film version "to strike back."

Screenplay award at the 1974 Cannes Film Festival in France. The award and the modest profits of the film convinced studio bosses to allow Spielberg to make another movie. Their decision turned out to be a very profitable one.

Soon after *The Sugarland Express* was released, Spielberg, the college dropout, gave a seminar to film students who were visiting Universal Studios. After the seminar, one of the youths asked Spielberg to look at his student film, and Spielberg gladly obliged. It had not been long since he was a student and had tried to get studio executives to watch his own films. The audacious student was Robert Zemeckis, who, thanks to the break Spielberg later offered him, went on to direct *Continental Divide* (1981), the *Back to the Future* series of films (1985, 1989, and 1990), and the Academy Award–winning *Forrest Gump* (1994). Spielberg has always felt it important to encourage new talent in Hollywood and is responsible for initiating the careers of many commercially successful Hollywood directors, including Chris Columbus (writer of *Gremlins, Nine Months, Mrs. Doubtfire,* and *Home Alone* and its sequel) and Joe Dante (director of *Gremlins* and its sequel, *The Howling,* and *Twilight Zone—The Movie*).

While wrapping up *The Sugarland Express,* Spielberg had read Peter Benchley's novel *Jaws* after finding it in Zanuck and Brown's studio offices. The producers had bought the rights to make the best-selling book into a movie for $175,000 (which included Benchley's fee to adapt the novel to the screen). In *Jaws,* a great white shark attacks residents and tourists in a New England seaside town. The mayor of the town wishes to keep the attacks a secret because he does not want the summer tourist season ruined. Police chief Brody (played by Roy Scheider), marine biologist Matt Hooper (Richard Dreyfuss), and the rugged old shark hunter Quint (Robert Shaw) pursue the gruesome creature, and the movie culminates in a brutal fight for their lives. After reading the book, Spielberg recalled wanting "to do *Jaws* for hostile reasons. I read it and felt I had been attacked. It terrified me, and I wanted to strike back."

Spielberg was 26 when he was assigned to direct the $12-million movie, which he insisted be shot entirely on location on Martha's Vineyard, Massachusetts. He thought that shooting the picture in big tanks of water would not make it look realistic enough for moviegoers. The residents of the Massachusetts summer resort chosen as the location for the fictional Amity Island were less than pleased to

have more than 150 cast and crew members invade their seaside Eden; their vehement protests ended only when they realized how much revenue the production would bring to local businesses.

Before Spielberg and his crew began shooting on location, they spent many months in preproduction. Preproduction is the planning stage of a movie, a time for writing and rewriting scripts, casting actors, find-

Although the shooting of *Jaws* on location at Martha's Vineyard, Massachusetts, had been extensively planned, no one was quite prepared for the ocean's moody indifference to the project.

53

ing locations—and, in the case of *Jaws*, building a shark. Spielberg had many ideas about the shark for the movie but ran into obstacles when he attempted to use real sharks; the actor considered for underwater close-ups with the shark refused to get in a tank with live sharks during his test run. Spielberg also discovered that special-effects people in Hollywood did not have any idea how to make a life-size shark.

Somewhat frustrated, Spielberg finally contacted the former head of Walt Disney's special effects department, Bob Mattey, and asked if he had any ideas. Mattey came out of semiretirement and created a 24-foot, one-and-a-half-ton polyurethane shark, nicknamed Bruce. There were three versions of Bruce—made at a reported cost of $250,000 each— one for underwater sequences and two others (one that moved from right to left and one that moved from left to right). Getting Bruce to maneuver in the water was not easy, even with 13 scuba-geared technicians hired to operate him. During an initial run, he sank like a stone. The hydraulic system that kept him afloat blew up on the next try.

The struggle to make Bruce stay afloat and swim was only the beginning of Spielberg's problems in making *Jaws*. He ended up sequestered on the island of Martha's Vineyard for 155 days. The film shoot, scheduled to last two or three months, ultimately took more than five. Although he insisted on the authenticity of shooting the movie on location, Spielberg admitted, "The ocean . . . was a real pain. . . . With all the planning we did . . . nobody thought much about the currents or anything at all about the waves." Other complications were labor disputes, equipment boats pulled apart by currents, script rewrites, and changes in the color of the water. Richard Dreyfuss, who played the young marine biologist Matt Hooper,

often yelled during filming in mock frustration, "What am I doing out in the middle of the . . . ocean when I could be back in civilization, making personal appearances?"

While other members of the crew left the island for short trips to the mainland, Spielberg refused to leave, believing that if he left he might never return. His drive to finish the film against difficult odds proved that he was a committed and passionate director. As Spielberg left Martha's Vineyard on the final day, he mimicked General Douglas MacArthur's farewell speech in the Philippines during World War II by declaring, "I shall not return!"

Another challenge in filming *Jaws* was the need for a great white. Actors refused to get into tanks with live sharks, and the first of several expensive polyurethane sharks sank.

55

Jaws was released in the summer of 1975, the same year that the Vietnam War ended, and it was an immediate success, a "blockbuster" in Hollywood terms. One critic stated, "*Jaws* . . . is part of a bracing revival of high adventure films and thrillers. . . . It is expensive . . . elaborate, technically intricate and wonderfully crafted, a movie whose every shock is a devastating surprise." The 27-year-old director's career and life changed forever when *Jaws* became the first movie to break the $100 million mark in rentals. It also became the highest-grossing movie to date, surpassing even the 1939 classic *Gone with the Wind* (if inflation is not taken into account).

Although Spielberg enjoyed great attention after *Jaws* was released, part of the movie's success could be attributed to the three actors who helped make it a hit: Richard Dreyfuss, Roy Scheider, and Robert Shaw. John Williams, who composed the tense, eerie music for the film, won his first Academy Award for Best Original Score. He and Spielberg would go on to create many other memorable movie-music collaborations in the years to come.

The Academy of Motion Picture Arts and Sciences honored the film with four other nominations (Best Picture, Best Sound, Best Original Score, and Best Film Editing), three of which it won. However, the Academy caused a scandal when it nominated the picture, but not the director, for an award. Although Spielberg and Universal Studios both believed that they had been intentionally snubbed by the Academy, the movie continued to pull people (and money) into the theaters.

Spielberg was now catapulted into directorial stardom, but he did not spend much time enjoying his newfound fame. The success of his first major feature film could easily have made the young director arrogant. However, according to one of the producers of his next movie, Spielberg had simply mastered his craft: "I think his films will change now as his experience deepens. In other words he's only going to get better." And, according to the critics and public, he did improve with his next film, *Close Encounters of the Third Kind*, which he had begun to work on before *Jaws* was even in the theaters.

Spielberg did not take much time out to enjoy the fruits of his labors, but he did find enough time to meet and fall in love with actress Amy Irving in 1976. Spielberg was immediately smitten by Irving, and the two began what would ultimately be a tumultuous decade-long relationship.

5 The Aliens Land

AFTER COMPLETING *JAWS*, which Spielberg admitted he "didn't have any fun making," the director turned his attention to two subjects that had fascinated him since childhood: space and alien life. His next movie would be one he made from his heart, one for which he had great passion.

Spielberg proposed a movie to producers Julia and Michael Phillips (who ran an independent production company whose hits included *Steelyard Blues, The Sting*, and *Taxi Driver*) along the lines of many movies made during the 1950s about contact with alien life. Americans had been trained to gaze skyward after World War II to look for possible attacks from foreign enemies. Because so many people were looking at the sky, unidentified flying object (UFO) sightings increased and were even recorded by the U.S. Air Force. Spielberg had enjoyed such films

---

Originally titled *Watch the Skies*, Spielberg's film *Close Encounters of the Third Kind* drew on the post-war paranoia of Americans who scanned the night skies for German or Japanese invaders and instead began reporting UFOs. Here the ominous mother ship—in fact a 40-pound model—descends before astonished onlookers.

as *The Day the Earth Stood Still* (1951) and *Earth Versus the Flying Saucers* (1956) as a child. His ambitious teenage film, *Firelight*, was about scientists who observed mysterious lights in the sky—lights that, the audience is led to believe, are alien beings.

After completing *Jaws*, Spielberg spent the next two years writing the script for what would become *Close Encounters of the Third Kind*. The project's original name was "Watch the Skies," but Spielberg ultimately settled on the more technical term to clarify the story. A close encounter of the first kind is a UFO sighting, a close encounter of the second kind is physical evidence that UFOs and alien life exist, and a close encounter of the third kind is actual contact and communication with alien life. Although Spielberg paid homage to all the old alien pictures of the 1950s, his movie was a far more lavish project: it had a big budget, cutting-edge special effects, technically advanced equipment, and a script written by the director himself.

Once Spielberg finished the script, which is essentially about several reports of UFO sightings woven together into one story, Columbia Pictures, not Universal, decided to back the project. Throughout his career, Spielberg has worked with a number of studios, not wanting to be controlled by one organization. The film was budgeted for $8 million, but with all the special effects and locations, the film eventually cost $20 million to produce. Although movies often go over budget, it is unclear whether they will make back their expense. When *Close Encounters of the Third Kind* was released in 1977, both Columbia and Spielberg were happy with the box-office profits.

Spielberg's movie plays on the mystery of the phenomenon of UFOs, catching the excitement many feel about the possibility of alien life. Astronomer

Dr. J. Allen Hyneck, who wrote extensively on UFOs and served as a technical adviser on the project, claimed that even though the movie is fictional, most of it is based on fact. Spielberg ran into opposition from the air force and army and the National Aeronautics and Space Administration (NASA), which did not want him revealing any information about UFO encounters. He explained:

The Day the Earth Stood Still was one of many films Spielberg watched as a child that stimulated his fascination with the prospect of alien life.

Spielberg discusses a scene in *Close Encounters* with Richard Dreyfuss (left). A coup for Spielberg was casting French director François Truffaut (center)—whose manner and skill directing children Spielberg especially admired—as the scientist Claude Lacombe. The film also featured Bob Balaban (right).

I really found my faith when I heard that the Government was opposed to the film. If NASA took the time to write me a 20-page letter, then I knew there must be something happening. I had wanted cooperation from them, but when they read the script they got very angry and felt it was a film that would be dangerous. I felt they mainly wrote the letter because *Jaws* convinced so many people around the world that there were sharks in toilets and bathtubs, not just in the oceans and rivers. They were also afraid the same kind of epidemic would happen with UFOs.

Government consent or not, the film went into production, and everyone involved with the project kept very quiet about it. Spielberg wanted *Close Encounters of the Third* Kind to be a big surprise when it was released.

He set most of the film in average, suburban America. Although some sightings took the crew to places as far as India and U.S. national parks in Wyoming, the story of the central family in the movie, the Nearys, was set squarely in middle America, in Muncie, Indiana. The director wanted to make the point that UFO sightings are made by everyone, not just government officials and scientists.

The sets Spielberg envisioned required so much space that the production had to abandon California and work out of a dirigible hangar in Mobile, Alabama, that was about the size of two football fields and six times bigger than the largest soundstage in Hollywood. Production designer Joe Alves made the soundstage look like nighttime Indiana, where most of the story takes place. Spielberg was very pleased with the expert crew he assembled to work on the project, including Douglas Trumbull on special effects (he had worked on Stanley Kubrick's *2001: A Space Odyssey*), veteran chief cinematographer Vilmos Zsigmond, composer John Williams, and actor Richard Dreyfuss in the leading role as lineman Roy Neary. The film was shot in 1976, the year of the U.S. bicentennial, between May and September.

Perhaps the most memorable scene in the film is the final one, when the mother ship, with aliens aboard, descends upon a large group of curious onlookers and makes contact with them. The seemingly enormous, luminescent spaceship was in fact a 40-pound, six-foot fiberglass model built by Greg Jein. The aliens were played by 50 six- and seven-year-olds, and Spielberg often jokingly yelled on the set: "ETs! Stop fooling around!"

More impressive to some than the breathtaking image of the ship was the casting of preeminent French director François Truffaut, known for such films as *Jules and Jim* and *The Wild Child*, who had never appeared in a film other than his own. Spielberg cast Truffaut as the paternal and kind scientist Claude Lacombe because he felt the Frenchman combined qualities of a serious adult and a carefree child. Though Spielberg was initially intimidated by directing another director—especially one he admired so greatly—he found Truffaut easygoing and charming to work with.

Truffaut offered Spielberg some very important advice about directing children, advice that Spielberg has continued to follow throughout the years. The French director told him that children make perfect actors because they are so eager to please without worrying about doing a good or bad job and because they like to have fun. According to many reviewers, the child actors give some of the best performances in Spielberg's later films, including *E.T.* and *Jurassic Park*. Spielberg has stated several times that he feels most comfortable around children because they possess a certain innocent and wondrous quality that he himself has never lost.

In *Close Encounters of the Third Kind*, Lacombe heads a team of scientists studying the mysterious return of a squadron of American aircraft missing since the end of World War II. The crew members of all the planes are still missing, but the airplanes are in perfect condition. Viewers are later led to believe that the crews were abducted by aliens. Meanwhile, in suburban Muncie, Indiana, little Barry Guiler's toys begin to move on their own, and lineman Roy Neary, called out to investigate a power failure, is scanned by an object flying in the sky. Neary and Barry's mother, Jillian, witness police cars chasing what appear to be spaceships. The movie presents several other sightings around the world, while following separately Roy's

and Jillian's individual pursuits to find out more about the UFOs.

The flying objects emit a sequence of five notes, which scientists discover are the geographical coordinates of Devils Tower, Wyoming, the place where contact between humans and aliens occurs. When the mother ship lands, several aliens walk toward the awed humans. Neary is slowly escorted by the band of aliens onto their ship and looks back to smile one last time at the world of humans. There is no sense in the movie of hostility from the aliens, whereas in most

The spontaneous movement of little Barry Guiler's toys is only one of the early signs that humans are not alone in *Close Encounters*.

Shooting *Close Encounters* took the crew from Alabama to Indiana—and was done despite the nervous opposition of the U.S. Air Force, Army, and NASA, all of whom feared the effect of Spielberg's possible revelations about UFOs. The film ultimately won the Academy Award for Best Cinematography but still no recognition for Spielberg's direction.

previous films extraterrestrials had been portrayed as malicious beings intent on taking over the world.

Another acclaimed science-fiction movie, *Star Wars*, made by Spielberg's good friend George Lucas, had been released six months before *Close Encounters of the Third Kind* and surpassed *Jaws* as the highest-grossing movie of all time up to that point. After *Star Wars*, audiences seemed anxious for more space-related, science-fiction movies, and *Close Encounters of the Third Kind* offered them just what they wanted. The film received overwhelming critical praise, including these words from distinguished movie critic Frank Rich: "The freshness of the vision is contagious and exhilarating . . . almost childlike. *Close Encounters* is part of the celebration of innocence."

The Academy honored the movie with eight nominations, including one for Best Director this time, but the film only earned one prize, for Best Cinematography. Spielberg once again was snubbed by his filmmaking peers in the Hollywood community, who might have felt the 30-year-old director could wait to receive his Oscar. In 1980, three years after *Close Encounters of the Third Kind* was released, Spielberg made a bold move and reedited the film, cutting a few scenes and adding a new ending where audiences actually get to see inside the mother ship. The new version, called *Close Encounters of the Third Kind: The Special Edition*, brought both the director and Columbia Pictures additional financial rewards.

Many people wondered whether, after creating two of the highest-grossing and most widely seen movies of all time, *Jaws* and *Close Encounters of the Third Kind*, Spielberg could deliver another blockbuster. Before embarking on his next project, *1941*, Spielberg took a vacation and visited George Lucas in Hawaii. Lucas, whom Spielberg had known since 1967, spent six months vacationing in Hawaii after having made *Star Wars* to think about new projects. Both Spielberg and Lucas were exhausted from their recent film forays, which had put the young directors in the privileged position of making almost any film they desired.

The two began talking about collaborating on an action-adventure movie based on serials they had watched as children in the 1950s. Spielberg recalled, "At dinner one night, when George got the news that the film [*Star Wars*] was a hit the first week, and he was suddenly laughing again, he told me the story of these movies he wanted to make, a series of archeology films. . . . I've always wanted to bring a serial to life that blends Lash LaRue, Spy Smasher, Masked Marvel and Tailspin Tommy with elements of Edgar Rice Burroughs and George's great imagination." They believed American audiences were ready for an action picture complete with a larger-than-life hero, evil villains, exotic locations, and fast-paced adventure sequences.

Before Spielberg began seriously working on what would become the first of the Indiana Jones movies, *Raiders of the Lost Ark*, however, he directed a film in 1978 that made the money for *Raiders* less forthcoming than he had hoped it would be. Spielberg decided to direct *1941*, a comedy-action picture about World War II that ultimately bombed at the box office, after he read the script (by Robert Zemeckis, Bob Gale, and John Milius) and, he said, "laughed [himself] sick." A tale of an attempted invasion of Hollywood by a Japanese fleet during World War II, the movie, according to most viewers, did little besides exhaust the audience with too many subplots, ceaseless action, and would-be comic scenes that did not make nearly enough people laugh. Apparently what Spielberg found so funny on paper was impossible to translate onto the screen, but he tried anyway with a lavish and overblown production.

Spielberg maintains that the film is a comedy: in fact, his first feature-length attempt at the genre. However, he tried too hard to make funny something that was not, and audiences found nothing to laugh at. He recalled subsequently that while working on the film, "It was sorta like going in for X-ray treatments each day and you realize the cure is worse than the disease." One of the problems was Spielberg's use of comedians Dan Aykroyd and John Belushi to carry the film with one-line jokes in place of a well-told story. Spielberg had to cut a lot of the film, and Aykroyd later commented, "There were so many elements that had to be chopped out because the movie was so big, and [Spielberg] had to get it down to a manageable time." Spielberg also abandoned the use of storyboards to organize the movie; consequently, too many improvisations made the picture confusing.

The film did poorly at the box office when it was released in December 1979 for a number of reasons, one being that there was a national economic recession. People also did not want to see a film that joked about war while Iran was holding a number of Americans hostage. Furthermore, the nation was still coming to terms with defeat in Vietnam only a few years earlier. The American public did not want to be reminded of actual war, preferring escapist films like *Star Trek: The Motion Picture* and *The Empire Strikes Back* (the second movie in the *Star Wars* trilogy).

In his book *The Steven Spielberg Story: The Man Behind the Movies*, Tony Crawley wrote about moviemaking during the late 1970s: "That was the trouble with '78. Loons were in. The National Lampoon's *Animal House* syndrome had begun. It is still around, alas, with the *Porky's* films. Just why Steven Spielberg felt he had to join in with such unruly messes is one, the only, aberration in his career to date." Roger Angell reported in *Variety*: "The movie is too childish and impatient to stay with most of its events and far-out turns of plot long enough for them to yield many laughs, and the basic humor is a sock in the jaw followed by a kick in the groin . . . the impression of the picture is of a very high-budget high-school variety show." Most critics agreed that *1941* was one of Spielberg's worst movies.

After the disastrous *1941*, Spielberg returned to work on the project begun with Lucas in 1977, the film that would restore his career as a director. It took a little while for Lucas and Spielberg to find a willing studio for their script, written by screenwriter Lawrence Kasdan (the story was written by Lucas and director Philip Kaufman), but eventually Paramount

Pictures realized the powerful moneymaking potential of the two talented men. The studio agreed to finance the picture but not before threatening to impose heavy penalties if the project went over budget. While Lucas was working on the story for *Raiders of the Lost Ark*, he also wrote ideas for two other movies in the

After the flop of *1941*, Spielberg returned to the genre of action-packed adventure stories with *Raiders of the Lost Ark*, which he created with George Lucas. Here Indiana Jones (Harrison Ford) escapes from one of many exotic predicaments.

series, the prequel *Indiana Jones and the Temple of Doom* and the sequel *Indiana Jones and the Last Crusade*, all of which Spielberg would eventually direct.

Set in 1936, *Raiders of the Lost Ark* centers on a charismatic and adventurous archaeologist and professor named Indiana Jones. Jones was played by Harrison

Ford, who gained attention in Lucas's *Star Wars* as the character Han Solo and who would go on to star in the next two films in the Indiana Jones trilogy. In the movie, "Indy" searches for a mythical Ark of the Covenant, which supposedly contains the broken tablets of the Ten Commandments. Indy is a charming, romantic character who travels to exotic locations, falls in love with beautiful women, and triumphs over greedy villains and murderous headhunters.

While attempting to retrieve the Ark, Indy travels to such exotic destinations as Egypt and Nepal, but actual film locations included England, France, Tunisia, and Hawaii. Lucas wanted to make the film's tension level high with several action sequences, and Spielberg, after *Duel* and *Jaws*, knew how to make audiences sit on the edge of their seats. The offscreen star of *Raiders*, as of *Jaws* and *Close Encounters of the Third Kind*, is John Williams, whose musical score matches the film's breakneck speed and relentless excitement. But it was critical that Lucas, as producer, keep the project within budget, even if it meant restricting some of his friend Spielberg's ideas.

Spielberg stayed under the 87-day shooting schedule and $40-million budget because he continued to be intensely organized. He used storyboards assiduously (about 6,000 images in all), which allowed him to visualize the movie before cameras ever rolled. He believed it was very important to keep the film within its budget, at one point remarking, "It's hard to spend your friend's money." Spielberg wanted to reverse a trend in big-budget moviemaking, for which he was partly responsible. Spielberg said that he "looked at [his] favorite films from the 1930s and 1940s and thought how quickly and cheaply they were made." Thanks to Spielberg and Lucas's tenacious adherence to schedule, the film cost $20 million, half its proposed budget.

Filming began in June 1980 and lasted only 73 days despite the numerous locations. In one of the film's most popular scenes, Indy is confronted by a sword-wielding Arab in a crowded marketplace. In the original script, Indy was to use his bullwhip and fight the Arab to the death, but Ford, who was suffering from dysentery after eating local Tunisian cuisine (Spielberg brought his own food from the United States), was not strong enough for the fight. The script was amended, and Indy simply shoots the offender with his pistol.

Even though *Raiders of the Lost Ark* was an almost flawless shoot and an instantaneous success when it was released in 1981 (ultimately garnering eight Academy Award nominations and four Oscars), and even though it was encouraging for Spielberg after *1941*, he still did not believe it was a very personal film for him. He explained, "It's only a movie . . . not a statement of the times, the way things were in 1936. It takes all the license of an exotic entertainment that aims to thrill and scare and strike one with a sense of wonder—with the cleverness of the hero pitted against an enemy of despicable class and wit." Most believe the picture shows off Spielberg's moviemaking and storytelling skills, but the more poignant themes that had previously interested him—childhood, reconciliation, loss—are conspicuously absent.

Nevertheless, the idea for Spielberg's next film was born on the hot sands of Tunisia while filming *Raiders of the Lost Ark*. The small creature he imagined on those sands, while melancholy and lonely, would eventually inspire one of the most remarkable American films ever made.

6 E.T. Phone Home

SPIELBERG CAME UP WITH THE IDEA for *E. T. The Extra-Terrestrial* while he was filming *Raiders of the Lost Ark* in Tunisia, but he had been working up to his American movie classic about family, outer space, and extraterrestrials for most of his life. Tired of making huge, expensive movies, Spielberg now focused on a story about which he felt passionate. The director recalled,

> I remember when I finally sat down and wrote the idea for *E.T.*, it was in the Sahara Desert where I was working on *Raiders*. I was lonely with no one to talk to; my girlfriend [Amy Irving] was in California and so was George Lucas. Harrison Ford was ill and I wished I had a friend. Then I thought about being ten years old, which I've sort of been all my life, and about feeling like that. And I began inventing this little creature based on the guy who steps out of the mother ship in *Close Encounters*.

After a high-tension chase, E.T.'s rescuers deliver him to his mother ship in the film that was later called "the best Disney film not made by Disney."

At this point, Spielberg's busy professional life was taking its toll on his relationship with actress Amy Irving. The two spent a lot of time apart because of their hectic schedules, and when they were both home, as one friend recalled, "it was no fun to go over there, because there was an electric tension in the air. It was competitive as to . . . whose career [they were] going to talk about, or whether he even approved of what she was interested in—her friends and her actor life. He really was uncomfortable." Despite their love for each other, Spielberg and Irving parted in 1980, the same year she appeared in director Woody Allen's film *Honeysuckle Rose*.

While on location in the desert, Spielberg discussed his ideas for *E.T.* with Harrison Ford's girlfriend (and soon-to-be wife), screenwriter Melissa Mathison. As he told Mathison, "I found myself standing in the Sahara Desert . . . lonely and depressed, making this crazy movie [*Raiders of the Lost Ark*] with dust and airplanes and whips and snakes . . . and, indeed, something did fall out of the sky and hit me on the head in the shape of a small, fat, little, squashy character named E.T."

Although he initially employed writer-director John Sayles to write the script, Spielberg did not like Sayles's portrayal of the aliens as hostile to humans. So Mathison, whose previous work included *The Black Stallion*, eventually wrote the script for *E.T. The Extra-Terrestrial*, creating a story with the emotions and sentiments Spielberg had in mind. It was a tale of friendship between a lonely earthbound child and a 900-year-old alien who has been left behind, a story that Spielberg believed represented how he felt as a child: lost, lonely, alienated. Spielberg said, "[The film was] a personal movie for me, and closer to my heart than any movie I've ever made before."

Mathison's script focuses on Elliott (played by Henry Thomas), who feels different from everyone around him. His life in suburban America is bleak until he discovers the alien E.T., who is left on Earth when his companions, surprised by American scientists, flee in their spaceship; E.T. wants to return home. Elliott hides the alien in his bedroom, sharing his secret with his older brother and younger sister, and E.T. enlists the three children to help him construct a

Dispensing with his usual carefully formulated storyboard, Spielberg allowed the filming of *E.T.* to move more fluidly and emotionally. Here he directs Henry Thomas as Elliott, the boy who finds E.T. and hides him in his bedroom.

crude radar-communications system that will allow him to "phone home." Meanwhile, the U.S. government watches Elliott's home because officials believe it is where the alien is hiding. Close to death after being outdoors all night trying to communicate with his home, E.T. is taken prisoner by the scientists, who attempt to heal and study him. Elliott and the other children help E.T. escape, and after a suspenseful chase on bicycles the children reach the spaceship that will take E.T. home. The movie ends with E.T. and Elliott saying good-bye. The film thus shows a lonely boy and an equally lonely alien forming a bond that helps them fight and eventually triumph over the meddling, imposing world of adults.

Once the script was approved, Spielberg turned his attention to the technical aspects of the production, an area in which he was now considered a master. As one reviewer said, "No technical challenge appears to be beyond Spielberg." He was a genius at getting special-effects wizards and expert cameramen to see his vision of a film, and he excelled at bringing to reality the magical worlds imagined in his childhood.

Carlo Rambaldi, the Italian puppet-master who had designed the aliens for *Close Encounters of the Third Kind*, created the creature E.T. He constructed a live-action puppet complete with facial expressions and body movements. According to Douglas Brode, author of *The Films of Steven Spielberg*, Rambaldi initially hoped to create a single model that could do everything necessary:

> He and his team soon realized that this was impossible. . . . They set about creating three separate E.T.s . . . a mechanical model operated by cables, an electronic one for the close shots of precise facial movements, and a "walking E.T." for move-

ment sequences, operated from the inside. . . . Each E.T. was constructed with a skeleton of aluminum and steel, padded with a musculature of fiberglass, polyurethene, and foam rubber. . . . Spielberg insisted that when E.T. moved, it had to be clear "he's slow, not sure-footed; he's much more conditioned to a heavier atmosphere, a heavier gravity. He's a little clumsy on earth, always stumbling, getting knocked into by refrigerators, hitting walls."

Several actors operated E.T. from inside to bring the character to life: Tamara de Treaux, who at 2 feet, 7 inches tall and only 40 pounds was the shortest adult performer in show business; Pat Bilson, who was 2 feet, 10 inches tall; and a legless boy named Matthew de Merritt. Well-known actress Debra Winger, who won accolades for her film role in *An Officer and a Gentleman* (the number-four box-office hit of 1982), provided the voice for E.T.

When filming began in September 1981, 34-year-old Spielberg abandoned his career-long use of storyboards, fearing that he would limit himself emotionally if he blocked out the movie before starting to film: "I decided, this once, to take a chance. Just came on to the set and winged it every day and made the movie as close to my own sensibilities and instincts as I possibly could." The result of Spielberg's emotional output produced a film that some critics called "the best Disney movie not made by Disney."

The film was first shown to the public at the 1982 Cannes Film Festival in France. Richard Corliss of *Time* magazine wrote,

> Spielberg had brought his sci-fi romance to Cannes for its world premieres, and throughout the day he loped down the Carlton [Hotel] corridors dodging the dozens of would-be interviewers, photographers, and starlets, all cadging for a

moment with the world's most successful director. In the Palais des Festivals he heard the applause erupt throughout the screening and watched an audience of grim professionals laugh and cry after two weeks of wheeling and dealing. During the last minute of the film, the applause kept growing until the fadeout, when an exaltation of bravos enveloped Spielberg.

After Cannes, *E.T.* opened around the world to both critical acclaim and unprecedented box-office success; it was called a true American classic. A film about how love and friendship can redeem a life and make the world a safer place, it struck a chord—judging by the millions of viewers who went to see it upon its release by Universal Studios in 1982. Vincent Canby of the *New York Times* wrote, "E.T. is a slick, spirited comedy about children's coping in a world where adults have grown up and away from innocence."

E.T. was to become one of Spielberg's most personal projects in its poignant treatment of the friendship between a lonely boy and an abandoned extraterrestrial.

The movie soon became the number-one moneymaking hit of all time, grossing more than $700 million worldwide. (The only country that did not embrace the movie was Sweden, where the film was banned for portraying children as disrespectful to adults.) The movie itself cost a mere $10.3 million to produce, about 10 percent of which went into developing the creature itself. When the video was released in 1988, it instantaneously sold more than 15 million copies, making it the best-selling videocassette to date. The film earned nine Academy Award nominations, but ultimately won only three. Once again Spielberg had been nominated for, but not honored with, one of Hollywood's highest commendations, the award for Best Director.

What was the key to *E. T.*'s overwhelming success? How could, in the words of the director, a "small, fat, little, squashy character," capture the imaginations and hearts of so many? Very few people left the theater with dry eyes. "Towards the end of *E. T.*, barely able to support my own grief and bewilderment," said writer Martin Amis, "I turned and looked down the aisle at my fellow sufferers. . . . Each face was a mask of tears. Staggering out, through a tundra of sodden hankies, I felt drained, pooped, squeezed dry; I felt I had lived out a one-year affair—complete with desire and despair, passion and prostration—in the space of 120 minutes." By following his instincts and emotions, Spielberg had created a movie that spoke to audiences about separation, friendship, yearning, and hope.

During the same summer that *E. T. The Extra-Terrestrial* opened, Spielberg had another movie released: *Poltergeist*, which he wrote, produced, and helped direct with Tobe Hooper (who had directed *The Texas Chainsaw Massacre* in 1974). *Poltergeist* (the word describing a ghost that makes itself known by noises and rappings) tells the story of a suburban family, the Freelings, living in a house built directly over an old cemetery whose graves were allegedly relocated before the subdivision was constructed. When Steve and Diane Freeling have a swimming pool constructed, a bulldozer uncovers the graves of the old burial ground, unleashing terrible events.

Furniture and toys mysteriously begin to move and fly through the air; and the Freelings' youngest daughter, Carol Anne, becomes possessed by forces within the television set and is pulled into the netherworld. The Freelings retain professional parapsychologists who try to communicate with the spirit of Carol Anne via the TV. When they run into difficulties, a clairvoyant is asked to help save Carol Anne, and she explains that the spirits are in "a perpetual dream state, a nightmare from which they cannot wake. Inside the light is salvation. Carol Anne must help them cross over." Diane has to go into the netherworld to rescue her young daughter, and she succeeds in her mission. The Freelings decide to move out of the house, but during their last night there, the head of Carol Anne's doll falls off and her brother's clown doll attacks the boy. Diane finds herself crawling up the walls and over the ceiling of her bedroom. When she falls into the swimming pool, Diane is attacked by decaying bodies. The family finally escapes by car, stopping at a motel for the night. When Carol Anne turns on the television set, her father shoves it out of the room.

The movie is full of horrifying images drawn from Spielberg's own childhood fears, including the ominous clown, a dark tree outside a window, and a closet full of terrifying creatures. Whereas *E.T.* represented all the good things Spielberg felt or longed for in

childhood, *Poltergeist* represented all the fear and anger associated with nightmarish forces in the world. Spielberg told the media, "It's nice that I can release two sides of my personality in 1982. . . . *Poltergeist* is what I fear, and *E.T.* is what I love. One is about suburban evil and the other is about suburban good. One is a scream, and one is a whisper." Although *Poltergeist* did not receive the same critical or box-office success as *E.T.*, it nevertheless drew many people to the theaters. It also proved again that Spielberg could just as easily scare audiences as charm them.

The popularity of *E.T.* and *Poltergeist* helped make Spielberg one of the most powerful men in Hollywood. Tobe Hooper was a little-known director to whom Spielberg may have offered the position so

Bloom (Scatman Crothers) is delighted that the gloomy elderly residents of a nursing home have returned to childhood, in Spielberg's segment of *Twilight Zone: The Movie.*

After actress Amy Irving's surprise appearance at an airport in India, she and Spielberg reunited and tried to solidify their fragmented relationship through marriage.

that Spielberg could have as much control over the project as he wanted. The film contains Spielberg's trademark touches, technical mastery, dramatic images, and captivating special effects.

In 1982, Spielberg also coproduced the movie version of Rod Serling's famous television series *The Twilight Zone*. *Twilight Zone: The Movie* was divided into several segments, each guided by a different director. Spielberg directed the "Kick the Can" segment, which involved a melancholy group of elderly residents in a nursing home who surprisingly return to childlike states of behavior, eventually changing into cheerful children. Scatman Crothers, an acclaimed blues musician, plays Bloom, "an elderly optimist who carries his hope in a tin can," and who helps the old folks rediscover the child still within them.

Spielberg agreed to direct the next film in the Indiana Jones series because he longed to work with Lucas and his crew again: "I knew if I didn't direct, somebody else would. I got a little bit jealous, I got a little bit frustrated and I signed on for one more." He began scouting locations for *Indiana Jones and the Temple of Doom* in 1983, and while in India, Spielberg was surprised at the airport by Amy Irving, who was working on the film *The Far Pavilions*. The couple reunited, resuming their often tumultous relationship.

Indiana Jones and the Temple of Doom meanwhile began filming in the spring of 1983. A prequel, the film takes place in 1935, before the events in *Raiders of the Lost Ark*. Indy travels to Shanghai, China, where he meets Chinese gangsters in a nightclub and tries to exchange an urn for a diamond. There he hooks up with nightclub singer Willie Scott (played by Kate Capshaw), who is after the diamond herself. When fighting breaks out, Indy and Willie escape and are joined by an Asian boy, Short Round (Ke Huy Quan). The trio ends up drifting down a river into India, where they come upon a village being scourged after a sacred stone is stolen. Indy, Willie, and Short Round try to retrieve the stone and free the children being held captive in a palace in Bangkok.

Even more action-packed and fast-paced than its predecessor, *Indiana Jones and the Temple of Doom* delivers a predictable good-over-evil ending but contains enough violent scenes to have caused a controversy over its PG (parental guidance) rating. In late 1984, Motion Picture Association president Jack Valenti approved a new rating, PG-13 (for adults—with children under the age of 13 only admitted if accompanied by an adult). The new rating joined the four other production codes then in use: G (for general audiences), PG, R (for adults—children under 13 not admitted), and X (for adults only). (In 1990, the NC-17 rating—no children under the age of 17—replaced the X rating.)

Parents had complained about the violence in the film, and even Spielberg admitted that he would not want children under the age of 10 to see it. Particularly gruesome scenes show a priest tearing a man's heart out of his chest for use in a religious sacrifice, as well as people eating jellied monkey brains.

Like its predecessor in the series, *Indiana Jones and the Temple of Doom* was not a personal movie for Spielberg, who in many ways viewed his work on the picture as a favor to George Lucas. Critic David Denby of *New York* magazine (who had been an admirer of Spielberg's *Raiders of the Lost Ark*) wrote that the prequel was "heavy-spirited and grating. The frivolous treatment of child slavery makes you slightly sick. This lurid and gloomy trash goes on and on, without a joke anywhere, and it's not only sadistic and dumb, it's oppressively ugly. That Spielberg should devote himself to anything so debased in imagination is unbearably depressing."

Despite reviewers' criticisms, the movie became one of the top 10 box-office hits of all time when it was released in 1984, making more than $100 million. Spielberg himself did not think it was one of his better films. The movie, however, garnered two Academy Award nominations, for Best Original Score for John Williams and for Best Visual Effects, which it did win.

After *Indiana Jones and the Temple of Doom*, Spielberg wrote and produced several successful and

entertaining movies with Amblin, his newly formed production company, whose offices opened on the grounds of Universal Studios in Universal City, California, in 1984. Spielberg's goal in opening the company was to encourage and nurture not only his own projects but also the budding careers of other young Hollywood directors. *Gremlins*, directed by Spielberg protégé Joe Dante, was the first movie produced by Amblin. Spielberg's role as producer and executive producer (the person responsible for securing the money and/or the principal players of a film, the producer, director, and scriptwriter) would

Indy (Harrison Ford), Willie Scott (Kate Capshaw), and Short Round (Ke Huy Quan) encounter terrorized Indian villagers in *Indiana Jones and the Temple of Doom*, the second and more contentious installment in that series.

Spielberg and Lucas pretend to scuffle as they make their footprints in wet cement at Mann's Chinese Theater in Hollywood.

increase as he used Amblin as a center for developing other people's film ideas.

Although many productions were made with funds from large studios, Spielberg always enjoyed creative control, even while spending other people's money. After years of working within the studio system, he knew how to guide and promote the ideas of young filmmakers who were less savvy about the Hollywood system. During the summer of 1985 he helped launch *The Goonies*, for which he had written the story and was credited as co-executive producer, and *Back to the Future*, for which he was also co-executive producer. *Back to the Future* was directed by Robert Zemeckis, and *The Goonies* was directed by Richard Donner (who had directed the 1978 movie *Superman*). Both films did well at the box office and helped establish Spielberg as a formidable dealmaker as well as an outstanding director.

Spielberg's next directorial project was a departure from anything he had ever done before. Throughout his career he had been accused of not having the sensitivity to do character studies. "The biggest risk for me is doing a film about people for the first time in my career—and failing," he said in late 1985. Spielberg took up the challenge and found a new way to express himself in film.

Breaking the Mold

7

IN 1985 SPIELBERG EMBARKED upon a project that he dubbed his first film for adults—*The Color Purple*—about a poor young African-American woman and her experiences in rural Georgia.

Kathleen Kennedy, a friend and business partner of Spielberg's, had given him *The Color Purple*, a Pulitzer Prize–winning novel by Alice Walker. Kennedy had not given him the novel for consideration as a potential project but simply as a good book to read. Spielberg recalled,

> [Kathleen] gave me some background: "You know it's a black story. But that shouldn't bother you, because you're Jewish and essentially you share similarities in your upbringing and your heritage." I had some anti-Semitic experiences when I was growing up that Kathleen knew about, including prejudice and everything else that I had to go through at one particular high school. So I read the book and I loved it, but I didn't want to direct it. Then I picked it up again about a month and a half later, and I read it a second time. And I couldn't get away from certain images.

Spielberg directs comedian Whoopi Goldberg as Celie in *The Color Purple*, based on Alice Walker's novel. Spielberg's professed first film for adults, its African-American content seemed to many critics and viewers a surprising choice.

Some people were surprised that Spielberg, a white Jewish male, would opt to direct a story about a black Christian woman, but, perhaps for the reasons that Kennedy mentioned, he felt a connection with the story. In addition, when Spielberg asked coproducer Quincy Jones why they did not want to find a black or female director for the film, Jones replied, "You didn't have to come from Mars to do *E.T.*, did you?"

The now-seasoned director also believed it was essential that he continue to challenge himself. Spielberg had become a virtuoso at moviemaking long before his 40th birthday and feared he was in danger of doing films that were not daring or interesting enough to satisfy his own artistic yearnings. He believed that *The Color Purple* would be an ideal way to move away, at least for the moment, from action-packed, larger-than-life spectacle movies.

The Color Purple tells of two sisters, Celie and Nettie, who live in Georgia, are separated at a young age, and are eventually reunited many years later. It focuses on Celie's hardships: she is beaten and raped by the man she believes to be her biological father, who sends away the two children she bears him; she is later forced to marry Albert, who is as abusive as her father had been. Meanwhile her beloved sister, Nettie, becomes a missionary in Africa and sends Celie detailed letters about her life there. Celie in turn writes about her abuse to God. When Albert's former mistress, Shug Avery, comes to town, Celie and Shug become friends and protect each other. By the end of the story Celie has found the courage to become independent, and she is reunited with her children and her sister.

Spielberg met with author Alice Walker to discuss her ideas about bringing her novel to the screen, and

the two artists formed a strong bond. Spielberg was attracted to Walker's depictions of broken families and the ways characters cope with separation and loss; Celie embodies elements of loneliness and endurance, two qualities that often appear in Spielberg characters. Popular comedian Whoopi Goldberg was cast to play Celie after she auditioned for the part in Amblin's own custom-built theater. Two other notable celebrities cast in the movie were Danny Glover as Albert, Celie's husband; and TV talk-

Celie and Nettie's brutal separation by their abusive stepfather propels the story of *The Color Purple.*

93

show host Oprah Winfrey as Sofia, wife of Celie's son-in-law.

The film, released in 1985, dispelled the belief that Spielberg could only direct movies with outstanding special effects and children as stars. *Newsweek*'s David Ansen wrote, "*The Color Purple* triumphs over its own over-eagerness to please . . . the joy of the work, which rises out of the ashes of Celie's anger and oppression, shines through and overcomes the suspicion that one is watching the coloring-book version of Walker's book. When the women, all gathered around the dinner table, finally rise in rebellion against their men, it's hard not to cheer their declaration of independence as one's own."

But although many praised the film, it also had its detractors. Many in Hollywood believed that *The Color Purple* had trademark Spielberg qualities such as over-sentimental relationships between characters, insinuating that the director had failed to make a film with strong adult themes. John Powers of the *Los Angeles Weekly* criticized Spielberg's direction: "[He] has so little faith in his human drama that he tarts up every shot and pumps up every scene . . . bathes everything in the Spielberg-esque light that comes bursting through every window that isn't coated with lead. His zippity-doo-dah outlook reaffirms the very values Walker challenges." Some in the African-American community, meanwhile, accused the film of stereotyping black men as sexist and abusive. But in an interview, Whoopi Goldberg defended the film: "Sometimes black men in the movie abuse black women. Now people see lots of movies where white men abuse white women, and they never think 'This movie stereotypes whites.' "

Nevertheless, the film did fairly well at the box office. About this, Spielberg said, "I thought *The Color Purple* had a very low concept. I didn't think anybody would go to see that movie. . . . And I thought that was my art film. I thought, 'My God, it's got an all-black cast and all-black films have never really been that successful, except a couple of police pictures,' and so that surprised me." *The Color Purple*, though not a mega-hit like Spielberg's previous films had been, was showered with 11 Academy Award nominations but did not receive an Oscar. For the second time (*Jaws* being the first), one of Spielberg's films was nominated for Best Picture without his being nominated for Best Director. This time the snub from the Academy caused a significant stir in the Hollywood community. Warner Bros., the studio that released the film, put an ad in one of the movie industry's trade publications, stating, "The company is shocked and dismayed that the movie's primary creative force—Steven Spielberg—was not recognized."

Spielberg did eventually win the Director's Guild Award, but many viewed this honor as merely a consolation prize. The fact that he won the Director's Guild prize and not the Oscar is ironic because it is directors who nominate other directors for the Academy: his colleagues had praised him in one organization while snubbing him in another.

While filming *The Color Purple*, Spielberg had an experience that would forever change his life: 1985 saw both his marriage to Amy Irving and the birth of his first child, Max Samuel. (Ironically, Irving went into labor at the same time that Spielberg was filming Celie's childbirth.) Despite the birth of their child, however, the marriage was on shaky ground from the start. The edgy, unsettled quality that characterized their on-again, off-again relationship did not abate once the couple had wed.

After the controversial reception of *The Color Purple* and the birth of his son, Spielberg took a break

Spielberg expands his interest in space activity by helping to finance the Oak Ridge Observatory communications dish, which will scan wavelengths in space in search of alien messages. He stands before the dish with son Max and astronomer Carl Sagan.

from directing movies. He briefly returned to television work with the short-format series *Amazing Stories*. The experience was similar to his early TV work: every week the cast and story of each segment changed. Spielberg had a boundless imagination, and *Amazing Stories* offered him a relatively low-stress vehicle in which to express many of his ideas. He wrote 15 of the 22 shows for the series, but directed only 2: "Ghost Train" (aired in September 1985), about a train that collects dying people, and "The Mission" (aired in May 1987), about a World War II aviator on a bombing mission.

Because Spielberg wanted to spend time with his baby son, he did not launch any new directorial projects right away. While taking time off to consider his next project, he and his company, Amblin, continued to produce projects and promote new directors. He kept busy as executive producer to several movies, including *Young Sherlock Holmes* (1985), *The Money Pit* (1986), and the feature-length cartoon *An American Tail* (1986).

Spielberg had planned soon to film his own version of the Peter Pan story, with which he greatly identified, but he did not feel the time was right. Instead he decided to make another movie along the lines of *The Color Purple*, one that was based on a novel and was primarily driven by dialogue between characters but had action sequences as well. He believed he needed to do another dramatic film to establish himself as a director in that genre. He chose to base his next film on J. G. Ballard's 1984 book, *Empire of the Sun*, set during World War II.

Although his marriage to Amy Irving was already beginning to unravel, Spielberg once again threw himself into his work. He hired British playwright Tom Stoppard to write the script for *Empire of the Sun*, and the two worked together so well that Spielberg has subsequently employed Stoppard to read books and screenplays for consideration by Amblin. Spielberg also sought British actors to play roles in the movie, including the aspiring actress Miranda Richardson, who plays Mrs. Victor. (Richardson later went on to star in *Enchanted April*, *The Crying Game*, *Damage*, and *Tom and Viv*.)

The novel is a semiautobiographical story about Ballard's own struggles and loss of childhood innocence in China during World War II. The film begins in war-torn Shanghai on the eve of the Pearl Harbor bombing by the Japanese on December 7, 1941. The story is told through the eyes of young Jamie Graham, later renamed Jim by his wartime buddy Basie. Eleven-year-old Jamie (played by acting novice Christian Bale) is the son of a wealthy British couple and is fascinated by airplanes. One night in a hotel, Jamie accidentally signals a Japanese warship in the harbor to open fire on the city. A chaotic battle ensues, and Jamie is separated from his parents in the midst of street fighting; he returns home to find his house looted and in shambles. Jamie is discovered by an American truckdriver named Basie (played by John Malkovich) and eventually ends up in a Japanese prison camp. At the conclusion of the movie, Jamie surrenders to American troops and is finally reunited with his parents.

According to film critic James Monaco, "Spielberg's vision is no longer one of innocent wonderment; instead, *Empire of the Sun* concerns the end of inno-cence—a young boy thrown into adulthood and an entire generation thrown into an atomic age." In his film study on Spielberg, Douglas Brode quotes Spielberg as saying he had been intrigued with the idea in Ballard's book that a "child saw things through a man's eyes as opposed to a man discovering things through the child in him. It was just the reverse of what [he] felt was [in previous pictures his] credo."

Empire of the Sun, which was coproduced by Spielberg, Kathleen Kennedy, and Frank Marshall, was greeted with ambivalent praise and only moderate box-office returns when it was released in 1987. Many agreed that Spielberg was trying to deal with mature issues onscreen and that he was making good progress. In many ways, the character of Jim reflected Spielberg himself, who had had to contend with the traumas of an unjust world while growing up. After reading Ballard's book Spielberg also said, "I was attracted to the idea that this was [about] a death of innocence, not

Another venture into more mature, emotional subject matter, *Empire of the Sun* is about a boy's loss of innocence during World War II. Jamie Graham (Christian Bale) has unwittingly triggered a Japanese warship attack that destroys his home and tears him from his family.

an attenuation of childhood, which by my own admission and everybody's impression of me is what my life has been." Spielberg noted, "There are certain people in America who want to keep me young; that makes them feel safe. But I've had ten years, and a lot of success, in a certain genre of movie. Now I have to explore other forms, to shake myself out of what every artist fears, which is lethargy and apathy."

But Spielberg's next project was not one that moved him any further along his self-professed artistic

The final film in the series, *Indiana Jones and the Last Crusade* signalled the end of an era for Spielberg, who saw the series as pure entertainment. *The Last Crusade* appealed to him, however, for dealing with the broken and reforged bonds between Indy (Harrison Ford, center) and his father, Professor Henry Jones (Sean Connery, right).

path. Instead it was done as a favor to his good friend George Lucas, whom he had long before promised on a beach in Hawaii to complete the Indiana Jones trilogy. *Indiana Jones and the Last Crusade* was vital to restoring Spielberg's popularity and moneymaking ability after the financially disappointing *Empire of the Sun*. The new Indiana Jones adventure held great promise in earning lots of money for Paramount Studios, which backed the third "Lucasberger," as the Lucas and Spielberg productions were nicknamed.

Indiana Jones and the Last Crusade introduces a new character into the saga: Indy's father, Professor Henry Jones, played by Sean Connery. According to Brode, by having Connery—primarily known for his portrayals of the British spy James Bond (007)—play Jones

Senior, the director and producer were acknowledging that Indiana Jones was Bond's cinematic son. Spielberg was intrigued by the idea of the reconciliation of a father and son, yearning as always to come to terms with unsettled issues about his own father, Arnold. Spielberg had just turned 40, and his marriage to Amy Irving had disintegrated into a painful and much-publicized separation. He sought creative projects that would help him deal with the emotionally difficult situations in his life, and doing a movie about a father-son relationship seemed appropriate at the time.

The movie begins in 1912 in Utah with Indy as a young Boy Scout (played by River Phoenix). During a camping trip the boy Indy stumbles on villains who are looting the legendary Cross of Coronado. Indy tears the cross away from them and escapes, but they track him down and recapture it. Eventually, Spielberg cuts to the year 1938, when the adult Indy heroically regains the cross and has it put safely in a museum. His next adventure is the search for the Holy Grail (the cup that is believed to have held Christ's blood after his crucifixion and that is supposed to have miraculous powers). Indy's father, who is already close to finding the Grail, has been captured by the Nazis, and Indy tries to rescue him.

Indy is again played by Harrison Ford, and the movie is another hair-raising, action-packed adventure complete with Nazi spies and a clever villainess. Indy and his father find themselves in many precarious situations from which they always discover a narrow escape, arguing with each other at every turn.

When the filming of *Indiana Jones and the Last Crusade* was completed, Spielberg felt a great sadness about finishing the decade-long project with Lucas and the crew, genuinely believing he had witnessed the end of an era. As much as he felt the Indiana Jones movies were purely entertainment and moneymaking ventures, he still had had a good time filming them and had become very close to the people with whom he had been working.

Newsweek's David Ansen seemed to agree with Spielberg's sense of ending: "This thrice-told tale gives you your money's worth. Now it's time to hang up the bullwhip and move on." When the film was released in 1989, it was a great box-office success, as had been predicted, and Spielberg became a bankable director again.

The year 1989 saw the release of another Spielberg film in a different genre from *Indiana Jones and the Last Crusade*. Spielberg had always wanted to make a film like the great Hollywood romantic comedies of the 1940s, and he based his next film on the 1943 Spencer Tracy–Irene Dunne classic *A Guy Named Joe*, directed by Victor Fleming. The story tells of pilots Pete and Dorinda's love affair and how, when Pete is killed in a plane crash, his spirit returns to ensure that Dorinda gets her life back in order. Pete comes to terms with losing Dorinda by letting her fall in love with someone else.

Spielberg's adaptation, *Always*, was a bold attempt to combine a romantic comedy with fast-paced airplane action sequences. Spielberg had been thinking about the movie for well over a decade and had always envisioned Dreyfuss in the role of the smart-talking Pete, a flying firefighter. After Spielberg saw Holly Hunter in the 1988 movie *Broadcast News*, he knew she had the humor and energy needed for the part of Dorinda. Spielberg viewed *Always* as an intimate film and one that he found easier to make than any of the Indiana Jones movies with their far-flung locations, hectic action sequences, and large casts. Many critics believed, however, that the film's portrayal of an adult love affair rang false and that the situations in the film were unnecessarily over-romanticized. As film critic Leonard Maltin stated, "[It's] certainly entertaining but suffers from a serious case of The Cutes." Perhaps because Spielberg had recently separated from his wife, he focused on characters who were trying to make love work against adverse circumstances but ultimately could not win.

Spielberg and Irving's divorce became final in 1989, with Irving reportedly receiving a settlement near $100 million. Spielberg had begun a relationship with actress Kate Capshaw, meanwhile, whom he had first met in 1983 while filming *Indiana Jones and the Temple of Doom*. He and Capshaw lived together for several years before marrying in 1992.

Spielberg made a number of movies in the late 1980s, but several seemed to fall short of what the director yearned to produce: a personally and artistically creative film that would also earn the respect of critics and his peers. "Throughout the eighties," wrote Stephen Schiff in the *New Yorker*, "Spielberg's films often seemed like imitation Spielberg films, only preachier." In other words, in films like *The Color Purple*, *Empire of the Sun*, *Always*, and even the Indiana Jones films, Spielberg attempted a variety of different storytelling methods and moviemaking techniques but could not achieve what he was after.

While he was directing his films of the late 1980s, Spielberg was also working on projects that married computer technology with film for outstanding visual effect. *Who Framed Roger Rabbit?* released in 1988, coproduced by Disney's Touchstone and Spielberg's Amblin companies, and directed by Robert Zemeckis, mixed live actors with computer-generated cartoon figures. Set around 1947 in Los Angeles, the movie's

Roger Rabbit enlists the help of Detective Eddie Valiant (Bob Hoskins) in clearing his name of a Toontown murder, in *Who Framed Roger Rabbit,* a spectacular fusion of computer technology and live-action film.

human star, a private investigator (played by Bob Hoskins), looks into a murder in Toontown, the section of town where the cartoon characters live, like old Hollywood stars, in thrall to the big studios. Cartoon character Roger Rabbit, who is a big star and the prime suspect in the murder, hires Hoskins to help clear his name.

In 1988 Disney's chief, Michael Eisner, and motion picture head, Jeffrey Katzenberg, had great hopes for the success of their first combination live-action and animated feature. The film cost close to $38 million to produce, and as one Hollywood insider said, "It's unique and should be very successful. But when you're out that kind of money, it's hard to sleep at night."

Who Framed Roger Rabbit? charmed audiences, but critics had mixed feelings about the film. Richard

Corliss wrote, "Every framed frame is beguiling, as befits a pioneering project made by Robert Zemeckis ... and ace animator Richard Williams. But not all the gags—even those quoted from such Bugs Bunny classics as *Falling Hare* and *Rabbit Seasoning*—have the limber wit of the cartoons that inspired them. Nor do the human actors add much." But despite its shortcomings, the film gave moviegoers a sample of computer-generated effects never before seen by a mass audience.

Thus although Spielberg's films of the 1980s did not emerge unscathed by reviewers' comments, they helped the filmmaker mature and allowed him to experiment with different genres and forms. This experimentation—and perhaps the turbulence of his personal life in this decade—would prepare him for his seminal work only a few years later.

Peter Pan Grows Up

STEVEN SPIELBERG ENTERED THE 1990s with a career that few people could hope to achieve at the end of their lives, let alone at the beginning of their 40s. He had made some of the most successful movies of all time, had come through a difficult divorce, had found a new relationship with Kate Capshaw that brought him great happiness (they currently reside in Pacific Palisades, a section of Los Angeles), and was professionally in a position to make any move he desired. Now was the time to make the film he had thought about for a long time, the one that answered the question: What if Peter Pan grew up?

Spielberg had a new twist on the legend of Peter Pan. In his tale, called *Hook*, the evil Captain Hook is not killed by the alligator, as in J. M. Barrie's original dramatic fantasy of 1904. Peter, now an adult, must battle the nefarious pirate, who has kidnapped Peter's children from the nursery and taken them to Neverland. As actor Bob Hoskins

---

In his early 40s, Spielberg turned to the story of Peter Pan—Sir James Barrie's classic tale of a boy who refused to grow up—and invented a sequel, *Hook*.

(who played Smee, Hook's first mate) remarked, "*Peter Pan* is about lost childhood. *Hook* is about lost fatherhood." Spielberg was 44 when he made *Hook*, the same age as Sir Barrie when actors staged the first production of *Peter Pan*. Spielberg admitted that he identified with the boy who never wanted to grow up: "I've always been Peter Pan. That's why I wanted to do this movie."

Hook, conceived and created with high expectations and at a cost of about $75 million, had an all-star cast: Robin Williams as Peter, Dustin Hoffman as Captain Hook, Bob Hoskins as Smee, and Julia Roberts as Tinkerbell. And it had lavish sets, extraordinary makeup and costumes, and outstanding special effects—such as Tinkerbell flying effortlessly through the air and a bullet ricocheting more than a dozen times around Hook's pirate ship.

Audiences eagerly awaited *Hook*'s release during the Christmas season of 1991, hoping that Spielberg's sequel to the Peter Pan story would fill them with as much wonder and delight as Walt Disney's original version had. The stars alone should have ensured that audiences would flock to the movie. But *Hook* disappointed almost everyone who saw it. The story fails to have emotional impact: because the bonds between family members are never fully established, viewers do not become emotionally involved when Peter is reunited with his children. As a result, most critics judged the film to be "over-long, self-indulgent and shallow." Stephen Schiff sniffed in the *New Yorker* that *Hook* was Spielberg's "lumbering Peter Pan saga, which cost more than any other movie he had ever made, and which practically no one much liked." Vincent Canby of the *New York Times* wrote that "the movie's obviously expensive scale inhibits the fun instead of enhancing it." And Peter Travers of

Rolling Stone quipped, "The film has been engineered for merchandising potential and the widest possible appeal. What's missing is the one thing that really counts: charm."

Not all critics found *Hook* to be superficial, however. One of the few who uncategorically praised the film was George Perry:

> *Hook* confirms that there has not been a filmmaker since Disney who has such an instinctive feeling for the rapture and the magic of a child's imagination as Steven Spielberg. Quite simply it is the best kids' film in many years. For adults, it probes recesses of the memory that have long been papered over.

Despite the criticism, *Hook* satisfied Spielberg's longtime fascination with Peter Pan. And his next film, *Jurassic Park*, focused on another childhood obsession, dinosaurs.

In *Jurassic Park* (based on Michael Crichton's best-

Despite its twinkling effects and stellar cast, *Hook* was described by critics as "lumbering." Julia Roberts (Tinkerbell) and Robin Williams (Peter) regard their work with Spielberg.

Like his fellow computer-generated dinosaurs, this Tyrannosaurus rex dwarfs the presence of the human characters in *Jurassic Park*. Dr. Alan Grant (Sam Neill) faces the beast with Lex (Ariana Richards).

selling novel of the same name), billionaire John Hammond (played by the eminent British director Richard Attenborough) has created the ultimate adventure park on a tropical island. His scientists have recreated dinosaurs by extracting genetic material from the blood of a dinosaur-biting insect that was preserved in amber. Many species, such as *Tyrannosaurus rex*, *velociraptor*, and *apatasaurus*, among others, are on view in carefully guarded pens and cages. But things quickly go wrong in Jurassic Park when the electric fences keeping the dinosaurs in their cages are disconnected. Spielberg makes the message of the movie clear: the natural order of the world should not be tampered with, especially when fallible and greedy humans are involved.

As one critic said of the movie, "Steven Spielberg's *Jurassic Park* is nothing more—and nothing less—than the world's most extravagant Godzilla movie." It gave Spielberg an opportunity to employ the latest computer technology in bringing dinosaurs to life onscreen.

Stan Winston (who had worked on *Aliens*) designed life-sized action-model dinosaurs, researching scientic material to make sure his creatures were as close as possible to what paleontologists believe dinosaurs were truly like. Originally Spielberg had planned to use only life-size models, but after Lucas's crew—Industrial Light and Magic—joined, computer graphics played an important role. According to Brode,

> A breakthrough software program called Matador ... provided animators with an automatic sense of perspective, "brushes" which allowed for easy creation of shadows or smears of mud on a creature's back, and 16.7 million different hues for full verisimilitude of color. . . . [The] animator . . . could create the illusion that the dinosaur's skin was moving and his belly swaying. One look and Spielberg knew he had just seen the future; his film would be the first to include it.

Many wondered how the dinosaurs would look onscreen. *Time* magazine reported that they were "[a]mazing. Dinosaurs live. You are there, once upon a time, before mammal walked or man dreamed. You can pet a triceratops and, if you wish, examine its droppings." The critic David S. Jackson went on to report, "Spielberg loves to mix wonder with horror, and he has fun creating a living Museum of Natural History. . . . For dinosaurs to rule the earth again, the monsters needed majesty as well as menace. And Spielberg got it all right." Audiences shrieked with delight as Spielberg's computer-generated dinosaurs lunged and stomped on movie screens across the country.

But in his review of *Jurassic Park*, Richard Corliss of *Time* commented: "No film could be more personal to [Spielberg] than this one, a movie whose subject is its process, a movie about all the complexities of fabricating entertainment in the microchip age. It's a movie in love with technology (as Spielberg is), yet afraid of being carried away by it (as he is)." Perhaps a symptom of Spielberg's fascination with technology, however, is what many viewers believe to be the film's weakness: the actors in the movie are literally and figuratively overshadowed by the awesome creatures sharing the screen with them. Although critics and audiences were impressed by the special effects, they did not have much praise for the movie's human performances.

When *Jurassic Park* was released in the summer of 1993, it quickly surpassed *E. T. The Extra-Terrestrial* as the largest moneymaker of all time. Made at a cost of almost $100 million, *Jurassic Park* grossed $350 million in the United States and $800 million worldwide. As of early 1996, video sales and rentals continued to make it the best-selling movie of all time. The book *Jurassic Park* contains far more brutal scenes than the movie, many of which Spielberg excluded from the final cut, but the realistic dinosaurs' actions were violent enough to stir up a debate over whether young

children should see the film. Spielberg himself—by this time the father of five—said, "I do think this movie is inappropriate for children under 13," but he did not want his own children under the age of 10 to see it.

Before he had completed *Jurassic Park,* however, Spielberg turned his attention to the film that would become the most important of his career to date. He said, "Everything I have done up till now has really been a preparation for *Schindler.*"

Made for $23 million (much of it Spielberg's own money), *Schindler's List* is based on Thomas Keneally's Booker Prize–winning 1982 novel, *Schindler's Ark,* about German businessman Oskar Schindler, who

Oskar Schindler (Liam Neeson) tries to make a deal as part of his extraordinary plan to save 1,100 Jews from Nazi concentration camps in *Schindler's List.* The stark black-and-white format both accentuated the film's spare, close-to-the-bone story and finally freed Spielberg from the color-drenched, cartoonish quality of many of his earlier films.

saved 1,100 Jews from the Nazi death camps during World War II. Spielberg had owned the movie rights to Keneally's book for a little more than 10 years when he decided to make the film. He credited several events in his life with inspiring him to retell the harrowing story on film, the most instrumental being the birth of his son Max in 1985. Spielberg said, "I don't think it ever occurred to me that I was actually going to make this movie until my child was born. Through the decision I made to try and expose my kids to Jewish history, I really sort of reimmersed myself in Judaism."

Spielberg also wanted finally to overcome his own experiences with anti-Semitism during his high school years. The director recounted the anti-Semitic acts he had encountered: they "consisted of humiliation ... being hit, being struck, having pennies thrown at me during study hall and name calling. People coughing 'Jew' into their hand as they walked by me. ... No one leaped to my defense and I just remember it was like going to war. ... I felt as alien as I had ever felt in my life. It caused me great fear and an equal amount of shame." *Schindler's List* was thus a film that Spielberg directed to quiet painful memories from his past but also to remind the world of the horrific events that took place only five decades earlier.

Spielberg later told Cathleen McGuigan of *Newsweek,*

> My films have been made for you [the public]. ...
> Just like somebody makes a hamburger the way you want it. ... Now I go to Poland and I get hit in the face with my personal life. My upbringing. My Jewishness. Jewish life came pouring back into my heart. ... The camera has always been my golden shield against things really reaching me. I came to realize the reason I [made] the movie is that I

have never in my life told the truth in a movie.
My effort as a moviemaker has been to create
something that couldn't possibly happen. So people could leave their lives and have an adventure
and then come back to earth and drive home. . . .
If I'm going to tell the truth for the first time, it
should be about this subject. Not about divorce or
parents and children, but about this.

Thomas Keneally and Steven Zaillian adapted
Keneally's 1982 novel to create the script about how
industrialist Oskar Schindler saved Jews during the
Holocaust by employing them in his factory in
Krakow, Poland. Actor Liam Neeson was cast as the
imposing Oskar Schindler, a German-Catholic play-
boy-businessman, and Ben Kingsley portrayed
Schindler's compassionate Jewish accountant, Itzhak
Stern, who proposes to Schindler the plan to save the
1,100 Jews, presenting a path that will benefit the
enterpreneur without placing him in too much
danger.

In March 1993, Spielberg took the cast and crew
of *Schindler's List* to Poland in search of "truth."
Filming on location is always challenging, and Poland
proved no exception. The actors and crew of
Schindler's List were subjected to freezing temperatures
during the winter, an exhausting shooting schedule,
and harrowing reenactments of Nazi atrocities against
the Jews. The film required an enormous amount of
organization and effort; it had more than 126 speaking
parts; 30,000 extras; 210 crew members; and 148 sets
on 35 locations. The director wanted to shoot scenes
inside Auschwitz, the former Nazi concentration
camp, but too many people in the Jewish community
felt it disrespectful, and he was denied permission.
Instead, he built a mirror image of the camp's entrance
and shot a crucial scene of a train pulling into

In making *Schindler's List*, Spielberg said that for the first time he did not care whether the film—which featured brutal scenes of Nazi atrocities against Jews—lost money.

Auschwitz. The train actually pulls out of the real camp and into the movie set.

Spielberg shot *Schindler's List* on black-and-white film, a format rarely used for commercial movies today, because he believed the story would be more powerful if it were shown in stark whites, grays, and blacks; color could not convey the bleak message he wanted to express. As Susan Wloszczyna wrote in the January 26, 1994, issue of *USA Today*: "Spielberg has likened black and white to 'truth serum.' And *List*... has moments of stunning visual truth." Spielberg did not use his usual methods while making *Schindler's*

List: no storyboards, no cranes, no zoom lenses. Everything was pared down.

The film's appeal to audiences was never guaranteed, considering the disturbing and terrifying images Spielberg chose to include, but as he stated later, "I'm not interested in whether this film breaks even. . . . It's the first time that I honestly feel that."

When Universal Studios released *Schindler's List* in December 1993, it was the most critically acclaimed film of Spielberg's career. In his December 20, 1993, review of the film in the *New Yorker*, Terrence Rafferty wrote, "What Spielberg achieves in *Schindler's List* is nearly miraculous. It is by far the finest, fullest dramatic (i.e. nondocumentary) film ever made about the Holocaust." And Stephen Schiff, also of the *New Yorker*, wrote that *Schindler's List* is "a work of restraint, intelligence, and unusual sensitivity, and the finest fiction feature ever made about the century's greatest evil."

The movie was honored with no fewer than 13 Academy Award nominations, ultimately receiving 7 Oscars. After waiting nearly two decades, the director's colleagues and peers and the viewing public finally recognized Spielberg's outstanding achievement, handing him Oscars for both Best Picture and Best Director. After the Academy Awards ceremony, Spielberg said that winning the prizes was like drinking a cold glass of water after a long thirst.

Making *Schindler's List* quieted some of Spielberg's former demons, monsters that have haunted him since childhood. His good friend Jeffrey Katzenberg believes that "*Schindler's List* will wind up being so much more important than a movie. . . . It will affect how people on this planet think and act."

After making his seminal World War II film, Spielberg spent more time with his wife and five chil-

With 30,000 extras and 148 sets, *Schindler's List* was enormously difficult to film. And like the Atlantic Ocean while Spielberg shot *Jaws* nearly 20 years earlier, the Poland winter was both a crucial element in the film and a harsh opponent.

dren. In 1994 he opened a theme-park-style submarine sandwich shop called Dive! in Los Angeles, and he plans to construct more restaurants worldwide. He also kept busy with such activities as having dinner at the White House with President Bill Clinton and attending the Consumer Electronics Show in Las Vegas with his longtime friends Lew Wasserman and Sidney Sheinberg, both of the MCA entertainment company.

Soon after receiving the Academy Award for Best Director in March 1994, Spielberg and two of his close friends, record impresario David Geffen and former Disney executive Jeffrey Katzenberg, discussed the idea of opening a major Hollywood studio and

entertainment company. According to Richard
Corliss of *Time*, Geffen, former head of Geffen
Records, "has made stars of the Eagles, Guns N' Roses
and Nirvana on records, Tom Cruise in movies and
some singing cats on Broadway." He has been a feature in the entertainment world since the 1960s and is
today a multibillion-dollar businessman.

Jeffrey Katzenberg brings other strengths to the
trio's venture. In 1988, after heading production at
Paramount Pictures, Katzenberg's mentor, Michael
Eisner, hired the "maniacally driven" young executive
to revitalize Disney's ailing motion picture and TV
divisions. Katzenberg said of himself, "I am very
focused about setting goals and achieving them. From
absolute minutiae to moving mountains." According
to Corliss, "Katzenberg supervised the glorious revival
of animated features while at Walt Disney Co.,"
including *The Little Mermaid, Beauty and the Beast,
Aladdin*, and *The Lion King*. In August 1994,
Katzenberg left Disney, being "forced out after a nasty,
nearly patricidal struggle with Eisner to step into Walt
Disney Company president Frank Wells's position after
Wells died in a helicopter crash."

Spielberg, Katzenberg, and Geffen sparked their
plan for the entertainment company in October 1994,
in Washington, D.C. An article in the *New York Times*
on October 16 reported the plan for the cooperative
business venture:

> Hours after attending a White House dinner . . .
> Steven Spielberg and Jeffrey Katzenberg were in a
> passionate discussion . . . over the final details of
> their secret plan to form a new Hollywood studio.
> Even though it was 1:30 A.M., they decided to call
> their partner, David Geffen. As three of show
> business's most powerful players spoke, they quick-
> ly realized that weeks of personal uncertainty had

At the grave of the real Oskar Schindler in Jerusalem, the director embraces Liam Neeson upon finishing the film. This moment may have marked Spielberg's strongest sense of creative fulfillment until then.

vanished: they felt ready to announce their plans for a multibillion-dollar studio and entertainment company . . . . By 6:30 A.M., Mr. Geffen . . . had joined his friends for breakfast in Mr. Spielberg's suite. "We all looked at each other and said, 'Let's do it.' "

The trio named their new company DreamWorks SKG (Spielberg/Katzenberg/Geffen) in 1995. Spielberg is slotted to run the live-action film unit of DreamWorks and will fold his production house, Amblin, into the new studio. Geffen will head the music division, and Katzenberg will oversee animation and television production. According to *Time*, "The three DreamWorkers are stars with different temperaments." Tom Hanks, who received Academy Awards for Best Actor in both *Philadelphia* and *Forrest Gump* and who hosted the American Film Institute's Lifetime Achievement Awards ceremony on March 2, 1995, in which Spielberg was honored with the Lifetime Achievement Award, explained:

> David does business in an ephemeral, gossamer way.... Jeffrey is Mr. Bottom Line, Mr. Brass Tacks. He operates every meeting with a strict agenda; No. 1 on that agenda is that the meeting lasts 22 minutes. Steven has almost a cartoonist's point of view. He can draw anything on paper and make it come to life.

After announcing the company's title, the gentlemen then had to raise the money to get the business going. Each put in $33.3 million of his own money. For Spielberg and Geffen, the sum was "bus fare," but for Katzenberg, it represented his "entire net worth." The DreamWorks team traveled from Seattle to Wall Street to Europe in search of the $2 billion they needed to launch their corporation. Willing investors were not hard to find. According to Spielberg, "It's like stacking hour over Kennedy Airport." They secured a $1-billion line of credit from Chemical Bank, and Paul Allen, cofounder of the Microsoft computer company, offered $500 million (one-eighth of his net worth).

There are several other business alliances that the three men have sought to ensure that their company is at the cutting edge of new entertainment technology. DreamWorks signed a deal with Silicon Graphics Inc., a computer graphics company, with which SKG will "jointly develop a system for computer animation." Spielberg stated, "This alliance was almost inevitable in the formation of DreamWorks. . . . I had such a wonderful, and revolutionary, experience working with Silicon Graphics on 'Jurassic Park.' "

DreamWorks and the computer giant International Business Machines (IBM) also joined forces "to create a system that would allow them to store, transmit, retrieve and protect their computer-based products." The founders of DreamWorks hoped to create a digital studio, the next technological step in the evolution of multimedia entertainment companies. A digital studio is one where material—film, music, animation, and video—is readily available via such electronic avenues as the Internet, CD-ROMs, and other digital formats. The advantages of the digital format include easy access to information and unparalleled video clarity and audio quality.

The men who created DreamWorks have tried to predict the future of entertainment; thus their plan to build a digital studio. As Corliss has pointed out, this is very important because

> [t]oday, and tomorrow, any ambitious entertainment outfit must be an all-purpose, universal-joint conglomerate—for two big reasons. First, the media are converging, one on top of the other, even as the computer, phone line and TV screen are converging into the brave new integrated system of tomorrow. Second, the globalization of the U.S. entertainment industry is roaring forward unabated, making Hollywood an exhilarating, sky's-the-limit export factory

In April 1995 Edgar Bronfman, Jr., chief of the Seagram Company, acquired the entertainment empire MCA from the Japanese company Matsushita Electric Industrial for $5.6 billion. When Bronfman took over the company, Spielberg's mentors Lew Wasserman and Sidney Sheinberg ran MCA, Wasserman as chairman, and Sheinberg as president. The studio owns such entertainment companies as

Geffen Records (Mr. Geffen sold them the company in 1989) and Universal Studios.

The *New York Times* reported on April 5, 1995, "DreamWorks has said it will probably sign a production and distribution deal with MCA if the studio retains Mr. Sheinberg. Executives close to the company said such a deal could be worth $1 billion." Spielberg is very loyal to Sheinberg, who gave the director his first break at Universal in the late 1960s, and it was reported that "[i]f Mr. Sheinberg were forced to resign . . . Mr. Spielberg might also sever his relationship with MCA. That could scuttle a potential sequel to 'Jurassic Park.'" A sequel to Spielberg's computer-generated dinosaur film, the highest-grossing film to date, would almost guarantee enormous profits for MCA.

Then, in July 1995, shocking Hollywood, Disney bought Capital Cities-ABC for $19 billion, accomplishing the largest takeover in show business history. It is not clear yet what effect Disney will have on DreamWorks' deal with ABC.

DreamWorks has had little trouble attracting investors, but some people speculate on how long the venture can last. Sheinberg said, "These people have professionally married each other, and I wish them the best. Now the reality is that 50% of marriages in America end in divorce." The three men involved in creating the first major Hollywood studio in 50 years will have to keep focused and remain interested if they are to realize the full potential of DreamWorks.

Spielberg, although working very hard to establish DreamWorks, has voiced some apprehension about the pace of getting the company running. He said,

> We could have built this up over a 15-year period. Instead, we're trying to do it in a couple of years. After our first planning sessions, I thought about

how much easier it would be to start with a single film, make it, see how it does, and if it does well, do a second picture. That's the conservative, play-it-safe side that haunts me before I fall asleep at night.

The team planned several initial projects for the new company, including three live-action movies to be released in 1996. As of 1995, Spielberg hoped to produce 24 features by the year 2000, with no more than 10 films each year. Katzenberg, as head of animation, was preparing *The Prince of Egypt*, a story about the Ten Commandments, for a 1998 release. Reportedly the next animated feature after that will be *El Dorado: Cortez and the City of Gold*. Eventually DreamWorks will, according to its founders, employ as many as 500 people.

No final structure yet houses the studio, but Spielberg has done a series of drawings and architectural plans that include a velociraptor standing sentinel before the animation building that is topped off by a Groucho Marx-esque nose, mustache, and spectacles. Spielberg explained, "I laid out what I thought would be the perfect studio, based on 25 years' experience."

For Spielberg's part in the venture he also had to convince his wife that "his involvement wouldn't devour him." Katzenberg allegedly told Kate Capshaw that Spielberg would only work from 8:30 A.M. to 5:30 P.M., Monday through Friday. This schedule gives Spielberg time to spend with his children and pursue one of his great passions, video games. Spielberg and Capshaw planned to move to New York City in 1995, but he was so busy with the new studio that they put the move off indefinitely.

Two features produced by Amblin in 1995 proved that Spielberg's innovative moviemaking vision remained intact. *Casper the Ghost*, based on the cartoon of the same name, contains 43 minutes of computer animation. *Jurassic Park*, by comparison, included only six minutes. The *New York Times* reported on May 29, "Films of this sort are pushing the technological limits for innovations in the use of visual computing tools." Once again, Spielberg had incorporated the latest electronic tricks into his films.

The other Amblin film of 1995, *The Bridges of Madison County*, is very different. Based on Robert James Waller's best-selling novel of the same name, it features actress Meryl Streep as a frustrated midwestern farmer's wife and actor-director Clint Eastwood as

Spielberg turns the tables on a photographer as he poses with his sisters—(from left) Nancy, Sue, and Ann—and his mother, Leah Adler, when she was honored as "Mother of the Year" in 1995.

The triumvirate of DreamWorks SKG—Spielberg with the "manically driven" Katzenberg (left) and "ephemeral, gossamer" Geffen (right)—promises a brave new Hollywood studio and entertainment company.

a wandering photographer on assignment for *National Geographic*, who falls in love with Streep's character. Eastwood directed the film, which generally received more positive reviews than the book did.

Both movies enjoyed success at the box office, illustrating once again that Spielberg's projects show no signs of decreasing in popularity. Video sales and rentals of his other films, from *Jaws* to *Schindler's List*, have not abated, and each year more and more young people are exposed to the director's wide range of work.

By never relinquishing his wondrous and childlike view of the world or his optimistic outlook, Spielberg has offered audiences some of the most enduring and penetrating images in movie history: the sudden and terrifying emergence of the great white shark in *Jaws*, the hovering mother ship in *Close Encounters of the Third Kind*, E.T.'s enormous eyes, Indiana Jones's daring escape from a giant rolling boulder in *Raiders of the Lost Ark*, Celie's reunion with her sister in *The Color Purple*, and the horror of the Krakow ghetto in *Schindler's List*. While he dealt with his own nightmares and fears, Spielberg gave his audiences a way to cope with their own by making his messages universal and accessible through such simple themes as friendship and the triumph of good over evil.

Spielberg made his childhood struggles easier when he invited people, like the bully who picked on him as a child, to join in the act that made him happiest: making movies. From that point on, he never compromised his vision or abandoned his dreams. His films, even when dealing with alien and supernatural occurrences, convey honesty, compassion, and truth. Because of these traits, Steven Spielberg has become the most successful director of all time.

He comforts moviegoers with the idea that there is always hope in the world. Spielberg himself declared that his love for creating films comes from "wanting to make people happy from the beginning of [his] life."

Appendix ★ ★ ★ ★ ★ ★ ★ ★ ★ ★ ★ ★ ★ ★ ★ ★ ★ ★

FEATURE FILMS
DIRECTED

Duel.
Universal Television Studios.
1971 (television),
1973 (theater).

The Sugarland Express.
Universal. 1973.

Jaws.
Universal. 1975.

Close Encounters of the Third Kind.
Columbia. 1977.

1941.
Columbia/Universal.
A-Team. 1979.

Raiders of the Lost Ark.
Paramount/Lucasfilm. 1981.

E.T. The Extra-Terrestrial.
Universal. 1982.

Indiana Jones and the Temple of Doom.
Paramount/Lucasfilm. 1984.

The Color Purple.
Warner Bros./Amblin. 1985.

The Empire of the Sun.
Warner Bros./Amblin. 1987.

Indiana Jones and the Last Crusade.
Paramount/Lucasfilm. 1989.

Always.
Universal/Amblin. 1989.

Hook.
Sony Pictures
Entertainment/Tristar
Pictures/Amblin. 1991.

Jurassic Park.
Amblin/Universal. 1993.

Schindler's List.
Amblin/Universal. 1993.

FEATURE FILMS
WRITTEN, PRODUCED OR
EXECUTIVE PRODUCED

I Wanna Hold Your Hand.
Universal, 1978.

Used Cars.
Columbia. 1980.

Continental Divide.
Universal. 1981.

Poltergeist.
Metro Goldwyn
Mayer/SLM. 1982.

The Twilight Zone: The Movie
("Kick the Can" segment).
Warner Bros. 1983.

Gremlins.
Warner Bros./Amblin. 1984.

The Goonies.
Warner Bros./Amblin. 1985.

Back to the Future.
  Universal/Amblin. 1985.

Young Sherlock Holmes.
  Paramount/Amblin. 1985.

The Money Pit.
  Universal/Amblin. 1986.

An American Tail.
  Universal/Amblin. 1986.

Innerspace.
  Warner Bros./Amblin. 1987.

Batteries Not Included.
  Universal. 1987.

Who Framed Roger Rabbit?
  Touchstone/Amblin. 1988.

Back to the Future II.
  Universal/Amblin. 1989.

Dad.
  Universal/Amblin. 1989.

Back to the Future III.
  Universal/Amblin. 1990.

Gremlins II: The New Batch.
  Warner Bros./Amblin. 1990.

Joe Versus the Volcano.
  Warner Bros./Amblin. 1990.

Arachnophobia.
  HollywoodPictures/Amblin.
  1990.

An American Tail. II: Fievel Goes
  West.
  Universal/ Amblin. 1991.

Casper the Ghost.
  Universal/Amblin. 1995.

The Bridges of Madison County.
  Warner Brothers/Amblin.
  1995.

TELEVISION EPISODES
DIRECTED

1969-72 Night Gallery
        Marcus Welby
        The Name of the Game
        The Psychiatrists
        Columbo

1985-87 Amazing Stories:
        "Ghost Train"
        "The Mission"

TELEVISION MOVIES
DIRECTED

Duel. 1971.

Something Evil. 1972.

Savage. 1972.

Chronology ★ ★ ★ ★ ★ ★ ★ ★ ★ ★ ★ ★ ★ ★ ★ ★

1947   Born in Cincinnati, Ohio, on December 18. He is the first child of Leah and Arnold Spielberg.

1961   Wins a contest for the 40-minute, fully-scripted war film, *Escape to Nowhere.*

1964   His first full-length film, the 140-minute *Firelight*, premieres at a Phoenix, Arizona, movie theater the night before Spielberg's family moves to California.

1965   Spielberg's parents are divorced.

1968   Produces and directs the 35-millimeter short, *Amblin'.* The film catches the attention of executives at Universal Studios in Hollywood, California.

1969   Sidney Sheinberg offers Spielberg a seven-year contract to direct television shows for Universal. Spielberg drops out of California State College to work in TV.

1971   Spielberg makes first television movie, *Duel,* followed by *Something Evil.*

1974   First feature film, *The Sugarland Express*, is released. Spielberg is hired by producers Richard Zanuck and David Brown to direct the film version of best-selling novel, *Jaws.*

1975   *Jaws* is released and becomes highest-grossing film to that point in time.

1977   George Lucas's *Star Wars* is released in the summer, followed by Spielberg's *Close Encounters of the Third Kind.* The two young directors begin discussing a project that eventually becomes *Raiders of the Lost Ark.*

1979   *1941* is released by a joint venture of Universal Studios and Columbia Pictures. Receives a mediocre reception.

1981   *Raiders of the Lost Ark* is released. Spielberg begins work on *E. T. The Extra-Terrestrial.* Coauthors and produces *Poltergeist.*

<table>
<tr><td>1982</td><td>*E.T.* is released by Universal Pictures to great critical and box-office acclaim. *Poltergeist* is released the same year. Spielberg begins work on *Twilight Zone: The Movie,* during which actor Vic Morrow and two children are killed in a helicopter accident on the set.</td></tr>
</table>

1982   *E.T.* is released by Universal Pictures to great critical and box-office acclaim. *Poltergeist* is released the same year. Spielberg begins work on *Twilight Zone: The Movie,* during which actor Vic Morrow and two children are killed in a helicopter accident on the set.

1984   *Indiana Jones and the Temple of Doom* is released by Paramount in May. Outcry over the movie's excessive violence prompts new rating code, PG-13, which excludes children under the age of 13 without parental guidance.

1985   *The Color Purple* is released. Spielberg directs two episodes for *Amazing Stories* to air on NBC. Spielberg and Amy Irving marry and have their first and only child, Max Samuel.

1987   World War II epic *Empire of the Sun* is released to mediocre reception.

1989   The love story *Always* is released as well as the final installment of the Indiana Jones series, *Indiana Jones and the Last Crusade.* Spielberg and Amy Irving divorce.

1991   Spielberg's long-awaited version of the Peter Pan story, *Hook,* is released to slight praise.

1992   Spielberg and actress Kate Capshaw marry

1993   Spielberg returns to the directing spotlight with two of his most financially and critically successful films ever: *Jurassic Park* and *Schindler's List.*

1994   Spielberg wins Academy Awards for *Schindler's List,* for both Best Picture and Best Director. Begins developing ideas for a mega-studio with two close friends and associates, billionaire David Geffen and former top Disney executive Jeffrey Katzenberg.

1995   The new studio, still in the planning stages, is named DreamWorks SKG.

Further Reading ★ ★ ★ ★ ★ ★ ★ ★ ★ ★ ★ ★ ★

Brode, Douglas. *The Films of Steven Spielberg.* New York: Citadel Press, 1995.

Corliss, Richard. "Hey, Let's Put On a Show." *Time,* 27 March 1995.

Gelder, Van Peter. *That's Hollywood: A Behind the Scenes look at 60 of the Greatest Films of All Time.* New York: HarperPerennial, 1990.

Giannetti, Louis. *Understanding Movies.* 6th ed. Englewood Cliffs: Prentice Hall, 1993.

Hillier, Jim. *The New Hollywood.* New York: Continuum, 1994.

Kroll, Jack. "Close Encounter with Spielberg." *Newsweek,* 21 November 1977.

Mabery, D. L. *Steven Spielberg.* Minneapolis: Lerner Publications Company, 1986.

Masters, Kim. "What's Ovitz Got To Do With It?" *Vanity Fair,* April 1995.

Mott, Donald R., and Cheryl McAllister Saunders. *Twayne's Filmmakers Series: Steven Spielberg.* Boston: Twayne Publishers, 1986.

Sackett, Susan. *The Hollywood Reporter Book of Box Office Hits.* New York: Billboard Books, 1990.

Schiff, Stephen. "Seriously Spielberg." *The New Yorker,* 11 February 1994.

Siegel, Scott and Barbara. *The Encyclopedia of Hollywood.* New York: Avon Books, 1990.

Sragow, Michael "A Conversation with Steven Spielberg." *Rolling Stone,* 22 July 1982.

"Super Shark." *Time,* 23 June 1975.

Taylor, Philip, M. *Steven Spielberg: The Man, His Movies and Their Meaning.* New Expanded Edition. New York: Continuum, 1994.

Index ★

★ ★

Elizabeth Ferber is a freelance writer whose work has appeared in the *New York Times Book Review*, the *Washington Post*, *New York Magazine*, and other national publications. She is the author of several books, including a biography of Yasir Arafat and a novel (*Soon Lost*), and has co-written *The Walker's Companion*, a Nature Company guide. Ferber resides in Brooklyn, New York.

Leeza Gibbons is a reporter for and cohost of the nationally syndicated television program *Entertainment Tonight* and NBC's daily talk show *Leeza*. A graduate of the University of South Carolina's School of Journalism, Gibbons joined the on-air staff of *Entertainment Tonight* in 1984 after cohosting WCBS-TV's *Two on the Town* in New York City. Prior to that, she cohosted *PM Magazine* on WFAA-TV in Dallas, Texas, and on KFDM-TV in Beaumont, Texas. Gibbons also hosts the annual Miss Universe, Miss U.S.A., and Miss Teen U.S.A. pageants, as well as the annual Hollywood Christmas Parade. She is active in a number of charities and has served as the national chairperson for the Spinal Muscular Atrophy Division of the Muscular Dystrophy Association; each September, Gibbons cohosts the National MDA Telethon with Jerry Lewis.

PICTURE CREDITS

DATE			

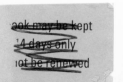

ook may be kept
14 days only
not be renewed

BAKER & TAYLOR